MIRACLES
of Hope

WHEN MIRACLES HAPPEN
True Stories of God's Divine Touch

Edited by Mary Hollingsworth

Guideposts
New York, New York

Acknowledgments

Every attempt has been made to credit the sources of copyrighted material used in this book. If any such acknowledgment has been inadvertently omitted or miscredited, receipt of such information would be appreciated.

All material that originally appeared in Guideposts publications is reprinted with permission. Copyright © Guideposts. All rights reserved.

Quotations designated KJV are from the King James Version of the Bible.

Quotations designated NASB are from the New American Standard Bible, © 1960, 1977 by the Lockman Foundation.

Quotations designated NIV are from The Holy Bible, New International Version. Copyright © 1973, 1978, 1984, International Bible Society. Used by permission of Zondervan Bible Publishers.

Editorial, research, and content development managed by Shady Oaks Studio, Bedford, Texas. Team members: Patty Crowley, Rhonda Hogan, Mary Hollingsworth, Mary Kay Knox, Kathryn Murray, Nancy Sullivan, Stephanie Terry, and Barbara Tork.

www.guideposts.org
(800) 431-2344
Guideposts Books & Inspirational Media Division
Illustrations by Ron Bucalo
Cover photograph by iStockphoto
Jacket design and photo by The DesignWorks Group, Inc.

Printed in the United States of America

Contents

CHAPTER 2   RESCUED BY HOPE

CHAPTER 3   HOPE COMES SOFTLY

CHAPTER 4 SURPRISED BY HOPE

CHAPTER 5   THE HOPE OF HEAVEN

Introduction

Emily Dickinson said, "Hope is the thing with feathers that perches in the soul, and sings the tune without the words, and never stops at all." To me, that means the hope of God is always there for us, singing through the darkness to keep our spirits up, a tiny light at the end of our tunnel, the glimmer of joy when sadness tries to reign. It's a miracle from the hand of God that lets us know we're never alone.

Some people believe in miracles; some people don't. But in reality, miracles are not about what we believe. Miracles don't cease just because we choose not to believe in them. God is God, and He can do anything He wants to do whenever He pleases. He doesn't need our permission or approval. And the miracle of hope in the face of life's disasters is proof.

How else can you explain a patient dying with cancer whose trust and faith become stronger day by day, not weaker? How else can you explain a single mother with three children and no money fixing a meal for someone else in need? How else can you explain a high-school football player giving up a promising career in order to donate a kidney to his dying grandmother? Hope is the answer—hope that, with the blessing of God, all will be well, no matter how the picture looks at the moment.

In *Miracles of Hope* you'll find yourself astounded as you share the true stories of people who have lost almost everything in life . . . except hope.

In Chapter 1, "On the Wings of Hope," Kate finds hope in her grandmother's christening gown. Vanessa is hit by a truck and, against all odds, lives to tell about the hope that pulled her through. And Luanne finds out she has a sister after more than fifty years of wishing and hoping for one.

David takes a leap of faith in Chapter 2, "Rescued by Hope," and by himself rescues three drowning people from torrential seas. Wendy receives a second chance at life. And Candy found spiritual renewal while undergoing six major surgeries.

"Hope Comes Softly" in Chapter 3 when Nancy finds a daffodil flourishing in a barren part of her yard—a symbol of hope through God's presence in her shattered life. Christy sees hope alive and well through her mother's quiet determination to walk again after almost losing her foot. And Charlie's hope is restored when a sermon he thought was inadequate saved a couple's marriage.

Nancy is "Surprised by Hope" in Chapter 4 when a

love banner she made to give her dad hope as he was dying also reignites her hope. Kathryn finds hope in a yard-sale prayer during the worst week of her family's life. And when everything seemed hopeless, Jan discovers her real mother . . . and her real hope.

In Chapter 5, "The Hope of Heaven," Kassandra races against time to pull a tiny boy from in front of a massive train. Emily's hope is refueled when God supplies exactly what she needed to keep her freelance writing job. And Betty finds her hope in the arms of her father when she thought she was lost.

As the old adage says, "When you get to the end of your rope, tie a knot in it and hang on." The knot in the end of our earthly rope is heavenly hope. It's what helps us hang on in the face of defeat, depression, and disaster. Join us now for a delightful dose of hope—you'll feel better after you do.

MARY HOLLINGSWORTH

MIRACLES
of Hope

Chapter 1

On the Wings of Hope

Those who hope in the LORD will renew their strength. They will soar on wings like eagles (Isaiah 40:31 NIV).

When life is tough, hope sometimes slinks away from us like a snake on its belly into the tall grass of fear. Without hope we struggle to cope with disappointment, defeat, or the uncertainty of unknown futures. Fortunately, when we refocus our thoughts and minds on God, we can soar above our problems and difficulties on the wings of hope, because hope comes from God—the Creator and sustainer of our lives, the One who holds our future in His omnipotent hands.

An Answer at the Truck Stop

KELSEY TYLER

D avid Hunter received the call just after nine on a Saturday evening in 1986 while on patrol with the sheriff's department in Knox County, Tennessee. A woman was weeping loudly in a corner booth at the Raccoon Valley Truck Stop. Several patrons had grown concerned and contacted the sheriff's department.

Hunter sighed and turned his patrol car in the direction of the truck stop. As a veteran officer of eight years, he had seen so much pain in the lives of people that he could only imagine what might cause a woman to weep aloud in a truck stop.

As he drove the remaining three miles, he remembered how pain was the reason he had joined the police force in the first place. He had ridden along with a police officer one night as part of the research he'd had to do for a local newspaper story he was writing.

The first call of the night involved a woman who had been badly beaten by her husband. Hunter watched as the officer handcuffed the man and led him away; he

3

saw the relief in the woman's face, and suddenly something clicked. He might write a thousand stories about good and evil in the course of a lifetime. But none of them could do for that woman what the police officer had just done. No story could rescue her from her pain.

Hunter began seeking police work the next day, and never once looked back. Now, eight years later, his love of his work was just as strong as it had been in the beginning. Despite the danger and frustration that came with the job, there were always nights like that one in which he could still make a difference for someone in pain.

Not sure what he would find, Hunter entered the truck stop cafe and immediately spotted the woman, still weeping, her face covered with her hands. Nearby sat two frightened little blond girls, ages about four and five.

Hunter's face softened as he approached the children.

"What seems to be the matter, girls?" he asked them. The older child turned to look at him, and Hunter could see she had tears in her eyes, too.

"Daddy left us," she said. "He put our stuff out of the car while we was [sic] in the bathroom."

Hunter's heart sank. He studied the woman, and gently placed a hand on her shoulder. Then he looked at the girls and smiled a warm, comforting smile. "Well, now, is that so?"

The children nodded.

"In that case I want you two to climb on those stools over there and order something to eat."

Reluctantly the girls walked away from their mother and took separate stools along the counter. Hunter signaled the waitress and asked her to get the girls whatever they wanted from the menu.

With the children out of earshot, the officer sat down across from the woman. She looked up from her hands and stared sadly at Hunter, her eyes filled with heartbreak.

"What's the problem?" Hunter asked quietly.

"Just what my girl said," the woman replied, wiping her eyes. "My husband's not cruel. Just at the end of his rope. We're flat broke, and he figured we'd get more help alone than if he stayed. I've been sitting here praying about what to do next, but I don't even have the money for a phone call. I just want to know God is listening, you know?"

Hunter nodded, his eyes gentle and empathetic. And silently he added his own prayer, asking God to show him a way to help this woman and her little children. He touched the gold St. Michael medallion he always wore around his neck. Although most police officers didn't spend a great deal of time talking about religion, Hunter knew few who did not rely on their faith. Many officers wore the St. Michael medallion under their uniforms because the archangel was recognized as the patron saint of warriors. Hunter believed with all his heart that God had indeed used angels to protect him in the line of duty on more than one occasion.

She needs an angel about now, Lord, he prayed silently. *Please help her out.*

Hunter broke the silence between the woman and him. "Do you have family?"

"The nearest is in Chicago."

Hunter thought a moment, and then suggested several agencies that could help her. As they spoke, the waitress brought hot dogs and french fries to the children, and the officer stood up and moved toward the counter. He took out his wallet to pay the bill.

"The boss says no charge," the waitress said. "We know what's going on here."

Hunter smiled at the woman and nodded his thanks. Then he stooped down to ask the girls how they liked their food. As he did, a trucker stood up from his table and approached the waitress. He mumbled something to her, and then she took him by the arm and led him to Hunter.

It was unusual for a truck driver to approach Hunter on his own. Typically truck drivers and police officers had something of a natural animosity for each other. Most truck drivers tended to see the police as cutting into their earnings by writing them tickets, while the police saw truckers as reckless people who placed their potential earnings before safety. The truth, of course, was somewhere in the middle, but still, Hunter couldn't remember a time when he'd been approached by a truck driver outside of the line of duty.

The trucker wore jeans, a T-shirt, and a baseball cap. He walked up to the counter and stood alongside Hunter. The officer noticed that the normal buzz of conversation and activity had stilled and the cafe was silent. Most of the patrons—nearly all of them long-distance truckers—were watching the conversation between the trucker and the officer.

"Excuse me, officer," the man said. "Here."

The trucker reached out his hand and gave the officer a fistful of bills. He cleared his throat.

"We passed the hat. There ought to be enough to get the woman and her girls started on their way."

Back when he was a boy, Hunter had learned that cops don't cry, at least not in public. So he stood there, speechless until the lump in his throat disappeared and he was able to speak.

Then Hunter shook the man's hand firmly. "I'm sure she'll appreciate it," he said, his voice gruff from covering up his emotion. "Can I tell her your name?"

The trucker raised his hands and backed away from the officer. "Nope. Just tell her it was from folks with families of their own."

Hunter nodded, and thought of the fiercely loyal way in which people in Tennessee looked out for each other. When the trucker walked away, Hunter counted the money and was again amazed. A small room of truck drivers had, in a matter of minutes, raised two hundred dollars, enough money for three bus tickets to Chicago and food along the way.

The officer walked back to the booth and handed the money to the woman, at which point she began to sob again.

"He heard," she whispered through her tears.

"Ma'am?" Hunter looked confused, wondering who the woman was talking about.

"Don't you see?" she said. "I came here completely desperate, hopeless. And I sat in this booth and asked God to help us, to give us a sign that He still loved us and cared for us."

Hunter felt chills along his arms and remembered his own prayer, how he had asked God to send help and provide this woman with angelic assistance. The truck drivers certainly didn't look like a textbook group of angels, but God had used them all the same. "You know, ma'am, I think you're right. I think He really did hear."

At that instant, a young couple entered the truck stop, saw the sobbing woman, and approached her without hesitating. They introduced themselves and asked if they could help in any way.

"Well," the woman said, "I could use a ride to the bus stop. See I've got the money now and I need to get to . . ."

Hunter stood up and walked discreetly away from the scene to a quiet corner of the truck stop, where he radioed dispatch.

"The situation's resolved," he said.

Then he walked toward his patrol car and climbed inside. When he was safely out of sight he let the tears come, tears that assured him he would never forget what happened that night in the truck stop. As a patrol officer, he had almost always seen the worst in people around him. But that night, he'd been reminded that kindness and love do exist among men. And Hunter had learned something else. Sometimes God answers prayer by using nothing more than a dozen big-hearted truckers sharing coffee at a truck stop in East Tennessee—and playing the part of angels.

The Gift of
the Angel Feather

KATE O'REILLY

It was 1998, and I was in the emergency room with a diagnosis of pneumonia. All the drugs used to combat this illness were given to me, and I was sent home with strict instructions on the importance of bed rest and taking my many medications. When I left the hospital, I felt I should really be staying, but there were no available beds. It appeared that, because of my age and general health, I would recover quickly on a homebound regime.

That evening, as I tossed and turned, being kept awake by the sound of the vaporizer, I finally fell into a very deep sleep. At 3:33 A.M. exactly, I was woken up by some presence in my room. At first I thought one of the other sick members in my family was up moving about. When I turned over in bed, my heart began racing. There in my room were two very large bodies. As I focused my eyes, my mind kept saying, *How could something this large fit into my bedroom?*

The two figures quickly made me understand without words that they were protecting me as I slept. I knew that they were angels. One of the angels was a male who stood about ten feet tall. But how could a ten-foot-tall figure fit in my room (which only had an eight-foot-high ceiling)? His robe was a very lovely blue-gray, and he had a loving face that felt healing to me. The other angel was all white. Her energy was soft and nurturing. She reminded me of the angels I read about as a small child: half feathers and half human. I reached out to touch them, and they were gone. I fell back into a restless sleep.

In the morning as I woke up, I became very excited about "the dream" I'd had about the angels. When my daughter and granddaughter came in to see how I was feeling, I told them about my visitation by the angels. My daughter was old enough to be skeptical, but my four-year-old granddaughter was awed and delighted by the story. After the excitement had passed, my daughter helped me out of bed to visit the rest room. At that moment, my granddaughter started screaming with excitement and glee. As I rose from the bed, a six-inch-long white feather came with me, stuck to my feverish leg! The three of us didn't know what to think. I was very confused because there are no feather products in our home due to allergies. My daughter was speechless, and my granddaughter was dancing with joy because the angel had left a gift. She said she knew the dream wasn't really a dream because angels visit people at night all the time. Of course it was an angel!

I carefully removed the precious feather from my leg and put it on my bedroom altar.

The next night, I felt that I was getting sicker, not better. I decided that if I didn't feel better soon, I would call my doctor. At 3:33 A.M., I was once again woken up by the feeling of a presence in my room. I turned over, and there were the angels again! As I watched them standing across from me, the male angel asked if I was ready to go with them to heaven. In many ways, I was overjoyed to hear them speak, and to invite me to join them.

The angels said they were there to help me decide whether or not I would stay living in my body. I thought about the projects I was working on, and about the unfinished business in my life. None of those things seemed more important than going with the angels. The love and contentment that they emanated was so appealing, and I wanted more of it. All of a sudden, though, I thought of my seven young grandchildren. All of my friends had said to me that they were here for a reason, and I could be a part of that reason. If I left with the angels at that moment, I wouldn't have a chance to at least say good-bye to the children and receive a final kiss and hug. I told the angels that I wanted to stay on the Earth plane for now.

The angels told me that if I were choosing to stay, the only way I could remain alive was if I went back to the emergency room quickly. They disappeared as suddenly as they had come to me. As soon as possible, my oldest daughter took me to the hospital. As it turned out, the pneumonia had gotten much worse, and the doctors said that I had made it to the hospital just in time.

The next morning at 3:33 A.M., I woke up, hoping to see my angels, but they weren't there. I wondered if moving to the hospital had confused them. I was very sad to think that I might not see them again, and I wondered how I might bring them back to me. I realized I should have asked them more questions. I felt that I had missed an opportunity, and I questioned my decision not to go with them. I cried, feeling as if I were mourning friends I'd had for years.

My daughter and granddaughter came to visit me later the same morning. I hadn't talked any more about the angels since the morning of the feather. I was too weak, just focusing my energy on getting better. My daughter also had a lot on her mind, and I didn't want to burden or worry her. As we talked about my hospital experience, my daughter remembered something from earlier in the morning. She said she had woken up at 3:33 A.M. and had gotten a strong feeling about an important decision she was trying to make. She was very puzzled by the fact that she had received such an insight in the middle of a sound sleep. But now her mind was made up—after many months of struggle, she finally knew what to do.

I smiled. My angels hadn't left after all; they were still with me and my loved ones. To this day, I cherish the gift of the angel feather.

The Christening Gown

KATHRYN LAY

I had been married only a few months when my grand-mother showed me the hand-made cotton baby chris-tening gown. It was off-white and had not yellowed or torn. Designed with delicate eyelet designs, I could imag-ine it decorating a porcelain doll. Or a precious child.

"Someday," she said, "I'll give it to you for my great-grandbaby."

I touched the gown and nodded.

My husband and I had dreamed of having three chil-dren. Our first child would be named Michael or Michelle, meaning "strength of God."

I knew my grandmother was excited about the idea of becoming a great-grandmother and I was excited about helping her to become one.

Three years later, after a disappointing time of many years of trying and hoping for a child, of anticipating pregnancies that never came true, my husband and I left the doctor's office to tell my grandmother that, at last, she would indeed be a great-grandmother in a few months.

She presented me with the gown, like a queen presenting a knight with his first suit of armor.

"Your great-grandmother made this while she was expecting me," my grandmother explained. "I wore it when I was a baby, my first time to be presented to God and society."

As the first-born grandchild and her only granddaughter, I felt a great deal of responsibility for the baby growing inside and the heirloom my grandmother so proudly passed on.

I put it in the room we would be using for a nursery. I had already begun buying little things in anticipation, finding a used dresser or changing table here and there. I lay the christening gown on top of the dresser we had painted yellow.

Two months later, I learned that my pregnancy had been an illusion, merely a desperate measure that my mind wanted so badly, telling my body to respond appropriately.

I cradled the gown in my arms, standing in the nursery we had begun. I felt as if I had failed as a wife and granddaughter. Would I ever hold a child, ever see it wear the gown? I cried until I felt I could never cry again. I had lost hope in ever holding my own child, in ever seeing my grandmother hold her great-grandchild.

Quickly, I gave away everything we'd bought. Friends who had babies on the way were better able to use them than we were.

But the gown was placed in a small antique strongbox. My baby hope chest. Beside it lay the solid gold earrings my mother gave me, passed on from her great-grandmother to the first daughter in each generation that married. I wore them on my wedding day, as my great-great-grandmother had done, a gift from her fiancé who had poured and molded them himself. I had hoped to pass them on to my own daughter someday.

Every so often, I would take out the gown and hold it in my lap. Eight years passed and I found myself unable to touch it.

My brothers had children. My cousins had children. I was grateful that my grandmother had not asked me to give the gown away, this special heirloom waiting for a small body to caress. Yet, I felt guilty holding on to it, holding on to a dying dream.

Then, in 1991, my husband and I began adoption classes. I often sat on the floor of the new future nursery, took the gown out, and wondered how my great-grandmother had felt in anticipation of her first child.

Michelle, my daughter, arrived in a flurry of joy and excitement. At nine months old, she had outgrown the gown before she had the chance to wear it. I bought a new dress for her baby dedication one December morning. My grandmother loved Michelle and never once showed disappointment in the christening gown not having been used for the purpose she'd given it to me.

Again, I put my grandmother's gown away.

Then one day, my three-year-old daughter came to me, proudly holding her snow-white bear that we had given her the day we first met her. The bear wore the christening gown. My daughter wore a smile.

"Look what I found. Isn't it pretty?"

I pulled both daughter and bear into my lap. "Yes, it's very pretty." I told her the story of the gown and our years of praying for a daughter like her. "Someday, I hope your child, my grandchild, will wear this special gown."

Michelle smiled at me. She carefully undressed the bear and put the gown back in the box.

Every so often, we take it out of the box and imagine the baby that will someday wear it. Yet, I've always wondered how my precious daughter would have looked in the gown.

This Christmas, my mother made porcelain dolls for each of her five granddaughters. The dolls were to resemble the girls. She allowed them to choose their doll's outfit.

"I'm afraid Michelle chose a pretty complicated one, my mother said. "I don't know if I can make it."

She showed me the pattern. "It's a christening gown," she explained. "Lots of eyelet lace. I just don't think I can do it."

My heart pounded. "I think I have an idea."

I slipped the gown from its resting place. Someday, I

felt sure a grandbaby or few would wear it. But for now, at last, I could see how my daughter might have looked.

I felt sure that my grandmother, who passed away five years ago when Michelle was three, would approve.

Hope in the Midst of Pain

VANESSA BRUCE INGOLD

Two weeks after my twenty-third birthday, I awoke to a foggy winter morning in Southern California. Having cried myself to sleep, I felt foggy too. Yet, dressed for aerobics, I began my usual bicycle route to the gym.

Since there was no bicycle lane, I pedaled alongside the parking lane of the four-lane business district roadway.

If it weren't illegal, I'd ride against traffic instead.

Ahead of me was a car in the parking lane. Just before I drew up beside it, the driver opened the door. I swerved.

Traffic noise seemed to intensify as I veered into the left-turn lane for oncoming traffic. Simultaneously, a Ford Ranger truck entered. I was trapped!

Scenes from my life flashed before my eyes, while my mind raced, *Will I be able to walk? Am I going to die? Will I go to heaven?*

Then the truck hit me.

Following the truck's piercing screech was a sound of a two-car collision. Debbie, the owner of a pet shop, ran to the sidewalk.

Instead of two cars, she saw the truck next to my smashed bicycle. I lay in a pool of blood.

Debbie called 911.

"She looks like a doll whose legs and arms are turned all the wrong way, the lower part of her left leg is like a balloon!"

Employees from other nearby shops encircled me. Debbie joined and directed traffic.

The man who had opened the door fled. Police questioned the truck driver. His truck, having left a brief skid mark, was damaged in the front and had to be towed.

Paramedics rushed me to Long Beach Memorial Hospital. All four tires had run over me. I was hysterically screaming and crying and was in and out of shock.

Wheeling me into the emergency room, they yelled, "Trauma code yellow!"

In one of my lucid moments, I said, "Call my friend Ray," and mumbled his phone number.

A nurse called Ray. He gave the phone number of the hair salon I worked. Next, the salon owner gave my emergency contacts. Then the nurse phoned my out-of-state family.

Heart surgeon, Dr. McConnell, entered. His eyes widened as he saw tire tracks going across my chest. My heart rate was 147, as if I were doing high-impact aerobics.

After evaluating, he said, "We've got to get her into surgery now."

During surgery, I had sixteen blood transfusions. They found gross, unstable blood in my abdomen; my liver severely lacerated; and my heart's papillary muscle ruptured, with my mitral valve ripped.

Every long bone in my body was broken except one, totaling 111. My lower left leg had the largest open wound, in which a fragment of the tibia—the bone that extends from the knee to the ankle—was sticking out of a six-inch longitudinal laceration.

Plus, many short, flat, and irregular bones were fractured, including knees, wrists, ankles, ribs, left clavicle, pelvis, and the C7 section of my cervical spine. A cervical collar was placed around my neck.

At 7:30 P.M. my family members arrived.

Dr. McConnell told them, "Her mitral valve is hanging like a thread, but we're trying to prolong replacing it because of the multitude of injuries and blood loss."

Relatives were allowed to see me. They and nurses laughed as I told a funny childhood story about my brother terrorizing me by putting my beloved stuffed animal in the freezer.

Laughter was interrupted. I had a heart attack.

"Now our only hope is to replace her mitral valve," Dr. McConnell explained.

Immediately a priest was sent to read me my "last rites." He asked if I understood. With closed eyes, I nodded.

After a ten-hour open-heart surgery, my chest couldn't be closed, because of severe pulmonary edema, coupled with edema of my heart. Thus, it was left open three days, covered with an Esmarch bandage. Paralyzing drugs kept me from moving.

After it was closed, I awoke with Dad at my bedside. *This must be bad if Dad's here.* My parents had divorced when I was in the first grade. We were not a close-knit family.

Since I was connected to a ventilator, I couldn't talk. My arms and legs were fixated with rods and pins. I had a feeding tube.

I cried. The metal attachments on my arms prevented me from wiping my tears. I was too weak, anyway.

I remembered having prayed the night before the accident, "Please change me, God."

Why'd You let this happen, God? Am I being punished for my out-of-control party life?

With tears on my face, I sensed Him reply, "It will all work together for good."

At least it can't get any worse; this is the worst thing that has ever happened to me!

But gangrene of my forefeet worsened. Still, oxygen therapy had to be postponed, until excess fluid that had accumulated in my chest was drained. With my legs elevated, I could see my black toes.

Two weeks after my chest was closed, I was brought to hyperbarics twice daily, where I was transferred into a single-person oxygen chamber that was seven feet long and twenty-seven inches wide. Each time, I was kept for one and a half hours, with hopes to save my feet and legs.

Two weeks passed, and I was told, "We'll be amputating all ten of your toes." Again, I nodded my head.

During almost four months in the intensive care unit, my ventilator alarm sounded because I lacked oxygen, a blood infection nearly killed me, and because of constant fever, ice packs surrounded me. Nevertheless, I witnessed God's love. My Christian trauma nurse visited me during her off hours. And a Christian family who met my family while I was having heart surgery, frequently visited me.

Trying to wean me off of the ventilator was a battle. Oxygen couldn't be reduced for long, because I panted.

"We're worried she'll be dependent on it forever," I heard doctors say. After nearly four months of dependence, a doctor was changing my tracheal tube. When she pulled it out and quickly tried to replace it, she couldn't insert the new tube.

"The incision in your neck has closed!"

Finally, I was independently breathing. An oxygen tank was placed next to my bed, yet I never needed it.

"Now you can begin rehab," a nurse said.

I frowned, "Rehab?" I breathily, hoarsely whined. "I

thought as soon as I was off the ventilator I'd be able to leave."

After a day in rehab, I questioned doctors. "You mean I broke over one hundred and eleven bones, had seventeen surgeries, and over one hundred blood transfusions?" *Wow, it really is a miracle I'm alive!* I began to see God's purpose for my life.

After a six-month hospital stay, on a clear, sun-shiny day, with a cast on my left leg, and two friends from whom I would be renting a room, I cheerfully left the hospital.

Six months later, a friend whom I had worked with at the hair salon invited me to church. Many there had been praying for me. The assistant pastor and his wife had visited me while I was in ICU, where they had anointed me with oil, while praying for my healing, as stated in the book of James.

Now I sat in the front row at church next to them.

After worship and Bible study, "Whoever wants to receive Jesus Christ as Lord and Savior tonight come to the front," the teaching pastor said. I stood and closed my eyes as he led in prayer.

The following Sunday, the pastor read from Romans chapter eight, "And we know that all things work together for good to those who love God, to those who are the called according to His purpose."

Wow, that's the Scripture of my life! What the enemy

had tried to use for evil, God was using for good. The accident had drawn my family together. Broken relationships were being rebuilt. Trauma was bringing healing.

A few weeks later, I visited my orthopedic surgeon, Dr. Peek. Ten months now I had had a cast. Hoping my tibia had finally hardened, again he shaved the cast off. Still soft, my tibia actually bent.

While he plastered a new cast onto my leg, I said, "I'm going up to the mountains today, for our church retreat. I'll just pray the whole weekend for God to heal it."

The following Wednesday, Dr. Peek announced, "Amazing—your tibia has hardened."

He never replaced the cast.

Eight years later, with a church group, I participated in a two-day bicycle trip to San Diego, a 110-mile ride. I rode thirty minutes behind, and was last to finish the ride. Although I'm not as fast, my hope will last!

Since then, I've had nine more surgeries. Yet, in the midst of pain, God has blessed me. Now life is especially more pleasurable since I have a cycling partner, my best friend and loving husband, Greg.

River of Tears

CAROLINE B. POSER

It was early February, the night of my older son's third birthday. I lay in bed, all wrapped up with him and his going-on-two-year-old brother, and cried a river of silent tears. While I had made it through Thanksgiving, Christmas, and New Year's Day just fine, this was one of the times that my divorce was really getting to me.

I cried for the shattered dream that was my marriage. My older son had been conceived on our honeymoon. I welcomed him into this world with such love and anticipation. I could barely take my eyes off of him—tiny little miracle that he was, co-created with someone I thought I would spend the proverbial "rest of my life" with.

I cried as I wondered, *Did I not try hard enough?* and *Should I have stuck it out longer?* and *Was it really that bad?* as my soon-to-be-ex-husband had asked me once.

I cried because I imagined that his pain must be just as real to him as mine was to me.

I cried because it really was "that bad."

For more than a year before I left I had been mourning the loss of my dreams. Sometimes I felt a ray of hope that things could be the way they used to be, that my husband had told me they'd be, that I wanted them to be —but those moments were fleeting.

I couldn't bear to look at any pictures from that year, because while they might have captured seemingly happy scenes, I knew how I felt on the inside. My mouth was usually set in a thin, grim line, lips pressed together tightly to prevent anything morose from spilling out onto my children or other innocent bystanders.

The duplicity was making me physically sick. I was grinding my teeth and had chronic headaches. My hair was falling out; I was tired all the time; and sometimes I felt as if I couldn't breathe.

When I began to feel that I would go insane, I started journaling. And when I realized I was writing the same things over and over and over: "I think I made a terrible mistake," "I'm so disappointed," and "I can't live like this," I knew the still small voice had spoken, whispering the truth in my ear. And then I couldn't hide from it anymore.

I cried because, as we all know, sometimes the truth hurts.

For a while, I had tried to put my feelings and my truth aside. But I knew in my heart that I wouldn't be doing my kids any favors by staying in a bad situation. And I realized I wasn't fooling them. I knew for sure that I had to leave my marriage when my older son studied me one day and said, "Mommy sad." He was not yet two and a half.

I cried because, even though one of my best friends had reminded me that everything happens for a reason, I couldn't imagine that this was really the way things were supposed to be. What could possibly be the reason that I should go through what I perceived to be so much pain and misery?

I cried because, as much as I wanted to wish I had never been married in the first place, I couldn't. Because then I wouldn't have the two wonderful boys dog-piled upon me, holding onto my hands with their own—one with long and slender Greyhound fingers and one pudgy, still-baby hand, reminiscent of a St. Bernard puppy.

I cried for these little boys who would never remember a time when their parents lived under the same roof, even though the logical part of my brain said, "So, who says it's not a family if it doesn't come in that particular 'nuclear' shape?"

I cried because I was sure that our having moved in with Grandma was a huge burden on her. We had descended upon her with a car load of belongings and two porta-cribs. She had generously moved out of her extra-large bedroom—which had at one time been two rooms—and into the smallish spare bedroom-office. We set up the porta-cribs on one side of the big room and I slept in Grandma's "big-girl bed" on the other side of the room, with sheets hung on a long wooden dowel to separate the two halves of the room.

I cried because we were all in the same bed together, which invariably wound up happening at some point during the night. Every night.

I sniffled.

Then I smiled—*because* we were all in the same bed together.

I sighed, because getting a good night's rest was difficult at best.

"Baby's kicking me," my older son would tattle, as if I didn't notice.

"He's kicking me, too, honey—please hold still, Baby!"

"Hee, hee, hee!" my younger son would exclaim with pure baby joy as he wriggled and snuggled in close, delighted to be in the big bed.

I regularly changed diapers (and sometimes sheets) in the dark and policed the bed to ensure everyone had a fair amount of bed, blankie, and Mommy.

And I chuckled, because even though I was physically and emotionally exhausted, it was hard to be grumpy when my younger son woke me up gleefully singing, "Ake op, Mama! Ake op!" And then he'd poke me in the face, labeling my features: "Ear." "Eye." "Nose." "Toof." "Air."

After all, this situation wouldn't last forever. The attic

renovation that would add a bedroom and office (scheduled to take one week but now going on three months) was nearly finished. (It had to be.) And then we'd have separate rooms.

I also knew that, while I counted on the support I was receiving from friends and family, one day—after losing just about everything I ever had, except my sanity, my children, and my ability to start over—I'd be able to stand on my own two feet again. I needed to be strong, because I knew that children handle divorce about as well as their parents. The demise of my marriage had brought me to my knees, and thus closer to God. In my weakness, I had found His strength. Maybe this was the reason.

As I lay in bed that night, two little bodies snug up against mine, the river of silent tears ran dry. And I recalled the words to one of my favorite hymns as I drifted off to sleep.

"I've got peace like a river . . .
"I've got love like the ocean . . .
"I've got joy like a fountain . . .
". . . in my soul."

Beautiful Flower

LUANNE HOLZLOEHNER

I used to play alone in my grandmother's gardens. I could almost get lost among the climbing blue hollyhocks and tall gladiolas. Even though I loved to play there, however, I always felt so alone. My mother died when I was three. My father didn't have much to do with me. Over the years I was shuffled around between stepmothers, a grandmother, and even an orphanage. And I was an only child. I had always wanted a sister. Throughout my childhood I was woefully alone. I had always felt something missing, a void so deep, longing for a sister. But it was not to be.

Playing in my grandmother's gardens, I used to imagine a sister, as beautiful as a flower. Someone to walk to school with me. Someone to read to me, and play with dolls. Still, I knew it wasn't real.

I grew up, got married, and had a family. I worked hard and had a good life and I was grateful. But sometimes, in the quiet of the evening as I was looking out over the vast green openness and the multitude of twinkling stars above, I still felt a strange longing for that connection only found in a sister. I hoped that somewhere out there, there really was a person who could make me feel complete. But I guessed God didn't really care about me all that much.

One night I was out on the porch in the stillness of the waning day, rocking gently, working a needle through my embroidery. Staring into the heavens, I felt that strange longing again. I was just about to go inside and get ready for bed when the phone rang. I dropped my sewing and moved inside.

"Hello?"

"Hello. I hope I have the right number. This is the Springfield police."

"Police?" I asked, bracing for bad news. Springfield, Vermont, was a town a few hours away where many of my relatives lived, and where I had gone to high school. But I hadn't been there in months.

"We have a letter here asking if we know the whereabouts of one Luanne Higgins," the voice continued.

Higgins: that was my maiden name. But I hadn't used it in years. I fidgeted nervously with the canisters on the shelf. "I'm Luanne. What is this all about?" I asked.

"It's from your sister," the police officer said.

Sister! I sighed and shook my head. Was this just a cruel trick? "I don't have any sister," I said at last.

"Well ma'am, they left a telephone number if you want to respond."

I had no idea what was going on, but I copied down the number anyway. I read the last name I had been given: Manley. It meant nothing. The phone number was in Maine. I knew no one in Maine. It didn't make a lick of sense. This must be a joke.

After two days of staring at that number on the slip of paper, however, I decided to call. One thought kept nagging at me. What if it was true? What if . . . ?

It took me hours to work up the courage. I kept looking at that phone and then I'd turn on my heels and walk away. Finally I picked up the receiver. I let the phone ring . . . one time . . . two . . . *This is ridiculous. I should hang up.* Three . . . four . . .

"Hello?"

Now what was I supposed to do? I stumbled all over my words. "Uh . . . this is . . . this is Luanne."

There was total silence. *Great! I've gone and made a darn fool of myself. This person has no idea what I'm talking about.*

Moments passed. Then, I heard a woman's voice, weak, almost a whisper. "Luanne? Oh my . . . Luanne! It's you! I've been looking for you for fifty years!"

I couldn't grasp it. "I'm . . . I'm sorry, I don't know who you are," I stammered.

The voice on the phone tried to explain. "I'm your sister."

It had been so long. No one had ever mentioned a

sister. I tried to wrap my mind around the idea. Oh, how I wanted a sister. But I almost couldn't let my heart hope that it could be true. How could I know for sure?

"I was eight years old when my mother married your father," the woman explained. "I remember the day you were born. You were so little. Mama and Daddy Bill didn't know if you'd make it."

The details of my birth weren't exactly normal. I was little—I had weighed only one pound. I had to sleep in a makeshift cradle under a light bulb for extra warmth. I had been told that much. Why hadn't I been told about a sister? Why didn't I remember?

"I used to play with you, and help take care of you. You were like a living doll! After Mama died, we stayed with my grandmother. But one day, I came home from school and you were gone. Daddy Bill had taken you away. I swore that some day I'd find you. And I've been looking for you ever since."

My mind swirled. So my father had separated us, and I was too young to remember. All my life I'd felt an emptiness, longing for a sister. And all this time I had one, searching for me. And I never knew. As much as I clung to this wonderful revelation, it still felt like a dream. I needed to see her to be sure it was real. I still felt like a little girl, pretending in my grandmother's garden.

We arranged to meet right away. My new sister offered to drive down from Maine and meet me at my home. That very weekend, I stood nervously on my porch as a dusty, blue minivan pulled up the driveway. I clasped my arms around my chest, as if to keep myself from falling into a million little pieces. The van had barely come to a stop when a tall woman with thick brown hair jumped out the door and ran toward me. My sister!

"Luanne!" she cried. She grabbed me and wrapped her arms around me, and I hugged her back. Sweet, warm tears streaked my cheeks. *Oh, thank You, God!* I'd waited a long time for that hug.

We spent the whole day talking and staring at each other. I had her curly hair. She had my nose. I didn't know very much about her, but already I knew in my heart we were connected. We were sisters. Finally I had that beautiful flower I'd always dreamed of in my grand-mother's gardens.

My sister's name was Rose.

Kelly's Angel

DEE FLEMING

My husband, Don, and I pulled into the high school parking lot that cold December afternoon. It had been twenty months since the shootings. Twenty months, and still I could hardly bear to look at that building.

Sometimes it seemed like only twenty minutes since the April day in 1999 when we waited with the hundreds of other frantic parents for our children to make their way through the cordon of police and emergency vehicles surrounding Columbine High School. Some of the kids came out crying, frightened, stunned. Some were rushed from the school in ambulances.

One teacher and twelve students, including our sixteen-year-old, Kelly, did not come out. For a day and a half they remained where they had died while investigators pieced together an account of two teenage boys who had fallen into the grip of a terrible evil—the evil that seemed to me to hover still about the place where it happened.

Like most of the others, Kelly was killed in the library, crouching beneath a table as bullets ricocheted through the room. *Just inside those windows!* I thought as Don got out of the car. Right behind that curved steel-and-glass façade. It was too much to bear. I turned my head away, unable to look.

It had been weeks before the examination of the crime scene was complete and police let the families visit the site. It was important to me to see the place where Kelly had tried to hide. I needed to pray at the spot, outlined in white on the floor, kneel where she died. But if I thought actually going to the library would ease its menace, I was wrong. The bullet-scarred walls, the splintered tabletops, a shattered computer screen— violence and hate were still palpable there.

We live just two blocks from the high school, and for a long time I could not even drive by it, taking long, bizarre detours for the simplest errands. But for Don's sake, and for our older daughter, Erin, I had to pick up my life again. And what helped most was remembering how Kelly loved angels.

From the time she was tiny, Kelly and I had shared a special affection for these messengers of God. I can still hear her piping little voice, at age three, reciting the verse on the little guardian angel card my mother had given her:

Angel of God, my guardian dear,
To whom His love commits me here,
Ever this day be at my side
To light and guard, to rule and guide.

Kelly loved that card. I'd often see it on her dresser top or catch sight of it with her schoolbooks. When she was older we would sit together on the sofa and watch *Touched by an Angel.* We never missed an episode. We bought the soundtrack CD too, and would sing along in the car, just the two of us.

For Kelly and me, angels were our shorthand for "God is near!" And His nearness is what made her such a happy child—a girl who woke in the morning with a smile and literally skipped through the day, blue eyes sparkling, long blond hair swishing behind her.

That's what gave the library its peculiar horror for me. Kelly was such a gentle, trusting little soul to die amid such evil! I'd given her a poem about angels that she kept in a frame on her bedroom wall. After she died I'd step into her room again and again and read it, lingering over one line especially: "Angels are with you every step of the way and help you soar with amazing grace." I wanted to believe an angel had been beside her that day, with her beneath that table, helping her soar above the terror.

Almost as though they knew I needed them, people sent angel figurines along with their condolences. They came from friends, neighbors, total strangers—china angels, metal angels, wooden angels. An eight-year-old daughter of a friend tried to count the angel images in our house one day and gave up at 175—and every one of those angels whispered to me that Kelly was fine.

Only around the library was I unable to feel comfort. Not that we hadn't tried to exorcise the evil from that place. The school district at first wanted to repair and refurbish the space, but Don and I and the other parents believed that no child should ever again be asked to study there. God brought us together in an organization we called HOPE—Healing of People Everywhere—to raise money for a brand-new library building.

What began as a fund-raising effort among the families was caught up by the whole community, then by the entire nation, and even beyond. The new school building was under construction now—Don had driven in that afternoon, as he often did, to check on its progress. "I'll stay in the car," I told him. I'd visited the building site with the other families just a few days earlier.

The new library posed no terrors. It seemed to me a sign of life continuing, life affirmed. It was the presence of the old site that continued to oppress and upset me. I glanced reluctantly at it through the car window.

Its exterior was unchanged, but inside, I knew, nothing was left of the old facility. Architects had come up with a design that preserved the cafeteria on the ground floor, while entirely removing the second floor where the library had been.

The cafeteria now had a spacious atrium feel, bright and light, with a beautiful mural of trees on the high ceiling, drawing the eye upward. Students and faculty of

Columbine High School had a space that all could enter without fear. With the other families, we'd see to it that no physical trace of the tragedy remained.

Yet for me, the place still menaced. I turned my back on it and stared the other way out the car window. *I need to know that Kelly's all right, Lord,* I prayed. *I need to know she's happy and at peace.*

Turn around. Look at the building. The nudge didn't come from me. That building was the last thing in the world I wanted to look at. I wrenched my head around . . . and blinked in astonishment.

Something bright was moving across those upper windows! Something shimmering and glowing, gliding slowly past the glass exactly where the old library had been. Open-mouthed I stared while the unmistakable figure of an angel hovered over that second story. Wings, radiant hair, flowing garment—no artist could have rendered a heavenly messenger of comfort more gloriously.

I sat awestruck, seeing, yet scarcely believing. Even here, even here! Your angel was here with Kelly, just as You are with her always and forever.

How long did the vision last—fifteen seconds? However brief the time on a clock, I knew the angel had given me a lifetime of assurance. In the midst of all the evil that ever was and ever will be, God is present. God is with us. God is stronger.

Charlie's Plate

KATHLEEN H. STARLING

Maybe you know the feeling. You're poking around at a garage sale or sifting through the stuff at a flea market when all of a sudden something just cries out, "Take me home!" It more than catches your fancy; it gets ahold of your heart. I know that feeling well. A little too well, according to my husband, Warren. "Kitty, you're too sentimental for your own good. If you keep bringing stuff home, we won't be able to close the door."

But that was before Charlie's plate came into our lives.

I found the plate at a flea market in Webster, Florida. It was seventy-five miles away from home but had great bargains. Warren claimed he was keeping an eye out for mower blades, but really he came along to make sure I didn't bring the whole market home with me.

It was good hunting. I found some beautiful carved figures for my living room and some antique kitchen utensils. It was getting late when I spotted a lady sitting on a blanket in the remotest corner of the market. The items on her blanket paled in comparison to others that day—sad castoffs even by my generous standards. But something caught my eye. A plastic plate with a child's drawing on it. It was not unlike a plate my daughter had made. This plate had a green stick figure, an uneven fence, and a big yellow sun floating in the sky. In the corner, in neat adult print: From Charlie.

How could a mother ever part with this? I thought, picking up the plate and running my fingers over the words. Someone was supposed to love Charlie's plate. I settled on a price with the vendor and tucked it into my tote bag. Soon as we got home, I hand-washed the plate and put it in the cupboard.

The next week my granddaughters Kelly, Megan, and Jami came to visit. I made the girls hamburgers for lunch. I reached in the cupboard for something to put them on. Charlie's plate!

"Today Grandma's got a very special plate for one of you to use," I said, holding up my latest flea market find. "It looks like something you guys might have drawn. The little boy who drew it was named Charlie."

"Grandma, what does Charlie look like?" Jami wanted to know.

"How old is he?" Megan asked.

"And why didn't Charlie's mommy want to keep the plate?" Kelly said.

"I don't know, girls, but we can make it our very own special plate," I said. "Who wants to eat from Charlie's plate?" All their little hands shot straight up.

Charlie's plastic plate was like fine china for the girls, and for the other seven grandchildren who came along later. Everyone wanted the privilege of using it. They were quick to learn the rules. Don't put Charlie's plate in the microwave. Never use a knife on it. Wash it by hand, not in the dishwasher.

We would talk about Charlie all the time. We decided Charlie was pretty smart and a good artist. "He even made the fence smaller, so it looks like it's off in the distance."

I wondered about Charlie. *Was he as cherished as his plate?* Sometimes I'd find myself thinking, *Lord, wherever Charlie is, please look after him. Love him and protect him.* I knew what Warren would say. I was getting way too sentimental. But that's the way I am. I get real attached.

One Saturday maybe ten years after I bought Charlie's plate, Warren and I decided to have a garage sale. Okay, he decided. Even I had to agree that it was time to let go of a few items. We put up signs around the neighborhood, then lined up toys and furniture and clothes the kids and even the grandkids had outgrown.

That afternoon, a couple wandered up our long drive. Warren immediately recognized the man.

"Kitty, this is Roger Dillard," he said. "He has an auto repair shop down the road in Saint Cloud. I used to get our old car fixed there, remember?" Roger introduced us to his wife, Carol.

Our house is on a lake, so we started talking about fishing.

"I guess you two must go fishing a lot," Carol said.

"Not me," I said. "I can't sit still long enough. But I like finding things around the lake. Come on, I'll show you." I took Carol to our back porch and showed her the fishing lures I had gathered over the years.

"That's a great collection," Carol said. "I'll have to tell our son about it. He's sick and homebound." Her words just hung in the air. I didn't know what to say. "I tell him stories about the people I meet, the people he can't get to see," she said, breaking the tension. Carol's eyes welled with tears. "I'm sorry. I don't know why I'm burdening you with all this. It's just that Charlie's been sick ever since he was three. Now he's eighteen, and the doctors don't give much hope for him. Charlie's so sweet. He's always telling me he wishes he could do something for me."

I really wished I could do something for Carol too.

We walked back to the sale in the front yard. Roger put his arm around Carol. "I guess we should be going now," he said. I watched them head down the drive.

"Wait," I called out. "I have something for you." I dashed inside the house, grabbed Charlie's plate from the cupboard and rushed back out.

"I want you to have this, Carol," I said. I thrust the plate in her hands. "I know your Charlie didn't make this for you, but I have the feeling he would have if he could. Please take it."

Carol stared at the plate. The strangest look came over her face. Without saying a word, she turned away and hurried off. I felt terrible about upsetting her more.

Later that evening the phone rang. It was Carol.

"I'm sorry I left so abruptly, Kitty," Carol said. "I guess I was in shock. I recognized my own handwriting. This really is my Charlie's plate."

Fifteen years earlier, she told me, the day Charlie was diagnosed with a brain tumor, a nurse came into his hospital room and gave him markers and papers to draw. The hospital was going to use the pictures for fundraisers for the children's ward. Charlie was so sick he could only do one drawing—a sunny scene, him standing by a fence. Carol jotted his name in the corner. That was the last time she saw the picture. She never knew it'd been transferred onto a plate.

"All these years the Lord looked after Charlie's plate," Carol said. "Just like he's looked after my Charlie."

Maybe the reason I love flea markets is not so much for the finds—it's for the stories. Each item I take home—whether it's an elegant figurine for my living room, antique utensils for my kitchen, or a plate for my grandchildren—has its own story for me to discover. A story beyond what can be imagined or hoped.

CHAPTER 2

Rescued by Hope

But now, LORD . . . my hope is in you (Psalm 39:7 NIV).

Life's journey is, without doubt, full of unexpected potholes, dangerous curves, and sideline ditches. The Bible says that if we stay on the "narrow way"—keep our lives between the ditches—we will enjoy eternal life. However, when we inevitably fall into one of those ditches, we can be assured that we will be rescued by the eternal hope we have in God. He alone is our Protector and Deliverer. Keep your hope in Him!

Leap of Faith

DAVID MICHAEL YODER III

The windows of the base operations room at the U.S. Coast Guard Air Station, Elizabeth City, N.C., rattled as 60-mph gusts from the worst storm of the year lashed the base. Staring silently into the rain-slashed blackness I was despondent—a feeling shared by the three other crewmen of our H-60 rescue helicopter.

We had just received word that three exhausted men were about to abandon hope as fierce Atlantic seas battered their disabled 41-foot ketch, the *Malachite*. This was what we were trained for, why our unit existed. But we couldn't help. The men were beyond our reach. The H-60 had a 300-mile operating radius and the sailboat was about 400 miles offshore. We could get there, but we would never make it back. The nearest ship was 10 hours from the sailors' position, and they wouldn't last that long.

I clenched my fists in frustration. This would have been my first offshore rescue mission. I had joined the Coast Guard because I wanted to save lives. But in my gut I felt the churning grasp of fear. Would I have been able to do it? As an aviation survivalman, I was trained to assist shipwreck victims. But I was a greenhorn. Lives could depend on me—and I was terrifed that I would fail.

Then Lieutenant Bruce Jones, our pilot, broke the silence. "Bermuda," he said.

Our heads snapped up.

"If we continued on to Bermuda we might make it," he said, excitement in his voice.

Bermuda was 620 miles from the base—the extreme limit of our helicopter's range. Even under ideal conditions, no H-60 had ever flown to Bermuda from the States. In the midst of a storm and stopping to hoist the sailors aboard, it would be touch and go.

After calculating our fuel reserve, we figured we would have 30 minutes to save the men. The H-60 couldn't land in the water. I would have to be lowered onto the deck of the sailboat and help the sailors into a rescue basket.

My heart pounded with excitement—and apprehension—as we took off into a raging blackness punctuated by jagged flashes of lightning. For two and a half hours the H-60 shuddered and pitched as the storm-fed gusts slammed into it. I could hear Lieutenant Jones and co-pilot LTJG Randy Watson over the intercom refiguring the distance and fuel calculation. They were convinced that our safety margin was narrowing. The winds and bone-rattling turbulence were even stronger than the forecast. But I was alone with my thoughts. *How can that boat survive this? Will I be able to get aboard to help them? Will it be afloat when we get there?* Below, like angry slashes in the blackness, were towering white-flecked waves. I thought of the worst scenario: The crew would already be in the water and I would have to go in after them. *Can I do it? Will I jump into those seas?* I felt cold sweat on my body.

Then we saw the boat. Illuminated in the beam of our searchlight was the *Malachite.* Shreds of her sails streamed in the intense wind. The boat hurtled down immense waves that loomed over her masts, which whipped back and forth. The crew radioed that they were taking on water. They wouldn't be able to stay afloat much longer.

As I sat in the yawning side hatch of the helicopter with my feet dangling over the side, my worst fears were realized. There was no way I could be lowered onto the boat's deck—not the way those masts were whipping. My fingers hurt from clutching the sill of the hatch. For the men to be rescued, they would have to jump into the ocean—and I would have to go in after them. Lieutenant Jones's voice crackled through the headphones in my helmet. "The boat's sinking, David. They want to go in. Will you do it?"

I hesitated. I didn't have to go and nobody would blame me if I decided not to. The blackness below terrified me. Cold sweat poured under my diver's dry suit.

The earphones cracked again. "I have to know now, Dave."

I looked down into the raging blackness. *God, what should I do?* I silently prayed. And the answer was immediate. I had a choice. Those men below had no options. I had always professed my belief in God. But I never had to prove it. This would be my leap of faith. I was their only hope. I turned to flight mechanic Dave Barber and nodded.

My headset crackled once more. "Thirty minutes, Dave. That's all the time we have."

I didn't need further explanation. The copter would leave in 30 minutes whether I was aboard or not. The rest of the crew couldn't be jeopardized for one man. My stomach was in knots, but I made my choice. I rode down in a sling and jumped.

As soon as I touched the water, the force of the sea tore me from the cable. While rising on the crest of each wave I frantically searched for the boat, hoping the survivors would be nearby. But the boat was gone.

Finally, in the glare of the chopper's searchlight, I spotted one man. We had wanted them to stay together, but the sea had torn them from one another. I figured I would never be able to reach all of them in time. But if I could save one, maybe two . . .

I fought to keep from becoming disoriented. Sky and sea seemed to merge, and at times I couldn't tell up from down. I struggled to the first man, then held onto him and snagged the rescue basket as it danced wildly at the end of its tether. After helping him in and giving the signal to hoist, I checked my watch. I had been down fifteen minutes. There was still time.

Then I was tossed to the crest of another gigantic wave—and spotted a second man. *Just a few minutes left, Lord. Give me the strength to get this one too.* I was tiring, and the sailor, in his weakened state, couldn't help much. I struggled to lift him into the basket. When he made it, I took a deep breath and tried to still my trembling hands.

I looked for the third man, but all I could see were whitecaps. *That's it,* I thought. *We were fortunate to get two.*

Suddenly the searchlight flashed through the flying spray. There was the third man! Although exhausted, I began swimming, feeling my remaining strength drain. *Could I get him into the basket when I reached him?* As I got closer, I wondered if he was even alive. Suspended in his lifejacket, he was bobbing in the waves. Then he rolled his head up and, with a haunted expression, looked me in the eye. My heart jumped.

I tried to lift him into the basket, but each time, I couldn't make it the last few inches, and we both splashed back into the water. Finally, with strength that was outside my own, I gave one last heave and he was in.

I had done it. *Thank You, God.* I thought the worst was over.

I glanced at my watch—five minutes to go. I signaled for the cable to come down without the basket. The way the basket had been flailing, it would be quicker for me just to ride the cable back up.

With two minutes to spare, I grabbed the end of the cable. But as I was about to be hoisted, a monstrous wave flipped me high in the air and spun me upside down. The cable snapped taut, leaving me entangled and underwater. For an instant I didn't think I would come back up.

But the fear was gone. I had made my leap of faith and had put myself in God's hands. *If You want me now, Lord, I'm ready,* I prayed.

Then the cable jerked, and I was out of the water and being cranked up toward the helicopter. Yet I was still not out of danger. As I watched helplessly, I saw the cable fray and unravel, until only one of the three strands remained intact. I was swinging wildly at the end of the tether, still 20 feet from the chopper, and 30 feet above the waves. If that third strand broke, I would be lost. There would be no way for the chopper to pick me up, even if I survived the fall.

But Dave Barber worked the frayed cable up to the door and wrestled me in. Relief washed over me as I settled back inside the helicopter.

"Great job, Dave," Lieutenant Jones's voice crackled in my headset. "Not bad for a first rescue."

After more than five hours in the air, we landed in Bermuda and still had over 50 minutes of fuel, thanks to a strong tailwind. When it was all over, we watched the video of our mission, and the scenes of those mountainous waves showed us just how big a miracle had occurred. The rescue operation had been beyond the ordinary human and mechanical abilities of our helicopter and crew. God had definitely been watching out for us and those men. And even though I had always believed in God, this really put the lid on it for me.

That meant I was a greenhorn no longer—in more ways than one.

A Second Chance at Life

WENDY JEAN STEVEN

Miraculous. That says it all. Plain and simple, I should have died. But God spared my life.

Just last spring I celebrated twenty-five years of marriage with my minister-husband and our three beautiful daughters. But in the fall of 1980 I lingered between life and death. My doctors told my parents it would take an act of God for me to survive.

At twenty-eight years of age, my future lay before me like an open road. In all honesty, I wasn't all that excited about traveling that highway. I remember telling my mom it really didn't matter all that much whether I lived or died. After all, I had no husband or children that needed me. And I could easily be replaced at work.

Although reasonably happy with my administrative assistant position in a Christian missions organization in Southern California, I was not happy with my marital status. Within a two-year period I had been in or attended the wedding of most every girlfriend I ever had. Each time I walked down the center aisle of a church in a different bridesmaid dress, I had a silent argument with

God. *Why haven't You brought Mr. Right into my life? Haven't you been listening to my prayers? Have I been destined to never know the joys of promising a lifetime of love at the front of the church?* I desperately wanted to be married. And while I had dated my share of suitors, there was not anyone currently on the radar screen.

While wrestling with the issue of singleness, I battled depression. From a biblical point of view I knew that singleness was a spiritual gift God gave to some. I knew it was definitely not a gift I wanted to be given. What I didn't know was how God would use a rather dramatic incident in my life to prove to me how much I really did want to live.

One morning in August as I was applying my make-up before driving to work, I noticed a small bump to the side of my nose. When I pointed it out to my parents a couple of days later, they suggested I have a doctor look at it. I followed their advice.

It was diagnosed as a run-of-the-mill cyst. Although it posed no danger to my health, the doctor knew I would be less self-conscious about my physical appearance if it was gone. He indicated that it could easily be removed through minor out-patient surgery. For the few weeks prior to the scheduled procedure, he prescribed me to take a common antibiotic. Given the cyst's close proximity to the brain, he wanted to thwart the possibility of infection.

Complying with doctor's orders, I took my daily dose of tetracycline. As I swallowed the little white pill with a glass of tepid tap water, I glanced at the calendar on the wall. Fortunately, it wouldn't be long until I could quit. I hated taking medications.

The surgery was a success. I was left with a tiny scar that would heal quickly. As a precautionary measure, my doctor doubled the dose of the antibiotic. He wanted to make sure my recovery would not be undermined by a secondary infection. Within a week, however, I was not feeling well.

At first I began to notice red welts all over my body. I called the nurse. When she asked me to describe my symptoms, I noticed they had faded. When she conveyed the information to the doctor, he didn't think it was worthy of concern.

Within a couple of days, the welts continued to show up. So did feelings of lethargy. Lacking my normal energy, I began to nod off after dinner while watching TV. By the end of the week I noticed I was having increased difficulty getting a deep breath. Feeling nervous, I didn't want to be alone. Although I only lived two miles from my parents' home, I opted to spend the weekend with them.

Come Sunday morning, when my condition failed to improve, my mom insisted that I be taken to the emergency room at the regional trauma center. The three-minute drive seemed to take forever. I was scared. Once examined, I was immediately placed in a room for observation. Within four hours my lungs collapsed, and I went into anaphylactic shock. Without the ability to breathe on my own, I was connected to a ventilator and total life support systems.

My pastor, having received a phone call, rushed to the waiting room to comfort my folks. He then slowly made his way past the nurses station to the room where I was camouflaged amid an array of tubes and cords. Wearing a sterile gown and paper mask, Pastor George called on God for a miracle. After that, I faded in and out of consciousness unaware of who was standing near me at any given time.

I do remember thinking, *Am I dying? Is this what death is like?* A warm bright light beckoned me. I was not afraid. I felt as though my mind was floating above my lifeless body. I could look down on myself.

I also remember one of my brothers coming into the room to encourage me to fight to stay alive. Dave told me that he loved me. He also told me that a bachelor pastor in Seattle I'd been corresponding with had called to say he loved me and would fly down if I wanted him to. I thought to myself, *Greg loves me? He'll come?* At that point I realized just how much I cared for the guy who dated my roommate a decade before in college. A small light of hope came on in my heart.

Although I wasn't afraid of dying and going to be with Jesus, I knew how my death would impact my parents and siblings. I didn't want to put them through such pain.

A team of fifteen specialists assigned to my case could not seem to stop the inevitable. At one point, one of my doctors came out to the waiting room, slumped in a chair, and said to my grief-stricken parents, "I'm sorry. We've done all we can, and we're losing her. If you are religious people, you'd better start praying."

Little did he know that the call to prayer had already literally gone around the world. As members of Wycliffe Bible Translators, my folks had notified their colleagues on every continent and alerted them to my plight. They had also alerted a friend named Mike from our church who worked in the pharmacy at the hospital where I was been treated. Mike pored over stacks of medical reference books in hopes of trying to find something that could guide my bewildered physicians. When I had been on life support for five days, he found something that seemed to account for the symptoms leading up to my hospitalization.

Although such a reaction was almost unheard of, it appeared I was allergic to tetracycline. Immediately the staff adjusted my treatment in response to what they now understood. Within a week I was breathing on my own. Within two weeks I was home and on the phone with the man who would propose to me twelve months later.

As I said, my life is nothing short of a miracle. My non-Christian pulmonary specialist said it best after I had turned the corner when he told my folks, "Something greater than myself intervened on your daughter's behalf.

A Heart of Hope

SUE FERGUSON

Stunned, I walked out the doorway of the medical office and into the hallway. Cancer took the lives of both my parents in their early fifties. The threat of that dreaded disease has hovered over me for nearly thirty years, but I never stopped to consider there might be something wrong with my heart.

Making my way down the hall, up the elevator, out the building, into the parking garage, up another elevator, and into my car I wondered what I would say to my husband. After all, he was expecting a call. *Will I cry?* Everything seemed unknown. Suffering from jetlag following a weekend speaking engagement, I had felt nothing but a little tired when I entered that building. Now, I felt sick, really sick!

Expecting a detailed report about the routine physical I'd scheduled, Randy answered his phone, "Hi, how did it go?" I could almost hear a smile in his voice; he anticipated a healthy report.

What should I say? I stammered, "The ultrasound showed calcification in an artery of my neck. The doctor said that usually if it's found in one place that means it's in others, and she showed me the slender oval on her screen. I asked if that meant I was more likely to have a stroke. 'Exactly,' she said." She seemed surprised I put that together, and I silently wished I hadn't. I continued, "And I failed the treadmill test."

The technician who conducted the stress test had responded to a couple of conversational comments I made by looking into my eyes and saying, "I don't usually share this, especially not with clients, but in my own family I am the only one who's lived past thirty-one." Just like a close friend, she comfortably shared her personal family health history of early deaths and heart stress until something about my results registered a need to stop and ask me how I was feeling. I noticed her own family story abruptly ended as she regained her professional aura.

"Fine," I'd answered when she asked how I was feeling, "Just hot, like a hot flash."

"You're hot?"

"Yes, but I'm fifty." *I get hot!* I felt fine but my stress level had gone up; as far as I could tell, not from the stress test, but from the inference that something was wrong—seriously wrong—with my heart. Our eyes never connected again.

During the consultation following the test, the doctor suggested I call my family physician and get a recommendation for a cardiologist. "In the meantime, you may continue your daily walks, but don't do any strenuous activity," she instructed with a smile. *What does she know that she's not telling me?*

My only visit to the family physician had been eleven months ago when we moved to the Atlanta area and I needed written permission to take advantage of the personal trainer my husband's employer provides.

I had liked her. Our new family doctor ascertained my family history quickly and ordered a mammogram. In the days anticipating that exam I felt miserable. Every ache and pain told me, *This is the time cancer will be discovered.* The lab called within twelve hours of my test and assured me they had reviewed my previous and current films and all was well. Instantly, my aches and pains subsided; I was healed.

But this time I was going to see the family doctor because I had flunked the nonstress test of my physical. I couldn't even guess what to expect. The receptionist scheduled the appointment immediately when I explained my abnormal test results. *Sure I wanted to get right in, but didn't she act like it was urgent?!* My fear only grew.

When the friendly doctor entered the examining room, I explained briefly, as though I needed to apologize for going to another healthcare facility, that everyone in my husband's office had raved about a place where you could have a complete physical for the $25 copay. I had gone.

She inquired about my experience. At the end of my summary I asked, "Did they stop me on the treadmill because I was hot?" *Because I get hot often and don't think a thing about it.*

"No," she replied. "They stopped you because your heart was stressed. You're lucky you didn't have a heart attack on that treadmill."

So, she'd said it! Or at least I heard, "You're going to fall over dead any second!"

She proceeded. "Start this medication today, take a baby aspirin each day, too, and don't do anything."

"Can I take walks?"

"No, I don't want your heart stressed."

What about the rest of me? I am stressed through and through! Tears filled my eyes and threatened to fall like Niagara, but I fought to maintain my composure. Quietly I said, "I know myself. I don't want this hanging over me."

Trying to calm me she said, "I know you're scared. I would be, too, if it were me, but there are worse things, and this is fixable. And trust me, with these results they're not going to waste any time seeing you. I'm calling to schedule the appointment now."

Was that supposed to make me feel better?

With each step up and down the stairs of our house

I wondered if I was going to keel over. Even my husband complained. "Sue, it's a little different now when you don't answer the house phone or your cell phone." Before, he assumed I was busy. Now . . .

The following day my husband sat with me at the heart clinic, waiting to hear my name called. All the emergency lights in the facility were blinking with an irritating bright, white light and at one point a siren briefly, but loudly, blared. *Are they attempting to cause a heart attack right here and now?* Finally I asked the nurse standing at the door calling my name, "Why are the lights blinking?"

"The fire alarm went off early this morning before anyone was here, and they haven't been able to get them reset."

Hmm, it's probably annoying her, too, but it's a health hazard for those of us with heart conditions. Do I? Could I really be here because I have a heart condition?

I sat uncomfortably on that paper-covered patient table pondering the thought of having a sick heart. Nothing about that patient room was comfortable. I couldn't lean back, there were no arm rests, my feet dangled, and I was tired—tired from restless sleep and fear of the possible prognosis. The bleak, boring room seemed to declare war on me. "You are so vulnerable and frail. You may eat healthy and walk regularly but (tauntingly) you are still here." The colorless room that was so void of personality seemed to strip me of mine. I felt helpless and hopeless in a body that seemed to be failing.

From the moment the cardiologist entered the room he seemed to be pulling for me. Even though the test results had brought about a whole surge of symptoms—sweaty hands, nervous stomach, numb and tingling arms, shortness of breath, insomnia, and a general feeling of overwhelming stress—I suffered no symptoms prior to the treadmill exam. He wasn't going to jump to any conclusions. The cardiologist took me off of the prescription my family physician had prescribed the day before and told me to continue the baby aspirin and come in the following week for a more specific test—this time they would watch a radioactive substance as it pumped through my heart. "No need to limit your activities," he stated seemingly amazed that anyone would rush so hurriedly to assume the worst. My husband and I left smiling and scheduled the test for the day he was to return from a business trip!

All seemed better until later when I weighed everything again . . . in the dark, alone.

The test had been flunked, my family doctor had told me I was lucky I hadn't had a heart attack, and I was still suffering from all my new symptoms. My husband was gone on a five-day business trip, and I would have to wait.

I don't like to wait! Waiting demands thinking. I'm

not a person who says, "I just never would have thought it could happen," cause if it can happen I've lived it in my mind and planned for every possible scenario.

Already it seemed I had run through the full scope of emotions and possibilities—stunned, scared, relieved, sick, healthy, impatient, afraid, denying, thankful, protective, and more. Why do my thoughts find it so much easier to linger over death than false positives?

God has taken me through similar situations in the past. Twenty-four years ago I was in a hospital room preparing for surgery when I gazed out the window to see a bird flitting by. God's care engulfed me as Matthew 6:26 came to my mind: "Are you not much more valuable than they?" (NIV). Three years later, shortly after the birth of my third child and my mother's miserable death with breast cancer, I discovered a lump. Fear struck but all was fine. Six years ago I was in ICU hovering between life and death; once again, God lovingly cared for me.

My three children are grown and I have been here to raise them and release them; now we are the best of friends. The husband from my youth has loved me for thirty years; he knows me better than I know myself. As busy as ever, I am free to spend my days doing as God leads. My life is full of love, adventure, and purpose! I'm no longer expecting to fall over dead with a heart attack, but if I did, there would be no reason for complaint. Wealthy I'm not! But when it comes to relationships with family, friends, and God, I am richer than any millionaire! And what's to come will be even better; heaven is sure to be beyond my ability to comprehend.

I'm too practical and realistic to assume the results of the next medical test will be perfect. I know they could be frightening; I may cry and pain may be on the horizon. But, perhaps the waiting has been good, because now I am ready.

For the past few days I've secluded myself. I ran comfortably to books that captured my interest and diverted my attention. But today I won't hide from my fear; I won't settle simply for a phone call with a friend. I will bare my heart—the core of who I am, not my blood-pumping organ—to my Father and rest peacefully in the comfort of His presence. I won't sleep away the afternoon, and I won't settle for easy distractions. Instead, my hope is placed in Him—my hope for today, my hope for tomorrow, and my hope for all eternity. And that, dear friends, is a miracle!

If You're There, God...
Can We Talk?

JAN COATES

Is this your son's wallet, ma'am?" the Missouri Highway Patrol trooper asked.

How did this officer find me?

Without directions no one could find my home, thirty minutes outside the city limits of Kansas City, Missouri, nestled within the back roads of Lone Jack, a small community that is home to a sparse population of farmers, professionals, and blue collar workers, most of whom enjoy the privacy afforded by miles of fencing, mature trees, and vast acreage spreads.

For me, my twenty-acre ranch provided seclusion and a retreat from my frantic work life. I knew less than a handful of my neighbors. As a sales and marketing professional, I measured my performance and corporate worth by my paycheck. I worked hard and kept my personal life to myself. All that my coworkers knew about me was that I was a newlywed with a teenage son from a previous marriage. I liked it like that.

Now, Trooper Marquart, standing on the ceramic tile foyer of my home, rephrased his question by saying, "Ma'am, are you Chris's mother?"

I tried to speak, but my body was already shaking and my lips quivering. Paralyzed words stuck in the bile-tasting lumps in my throat, while my heart pounded so hard it felt as if it would jump right out of my chest. As the danger alarms rang in my head, I didn't know whether to run, hide, or vomit.

Bill, my husband, finally, spoke up. "I'm Chris's step-dad, and Jan is his mother."

The officer nodded his acknowledgment before pro-nouncing his horrifying news. "There's been a bad wreck, sir. I'm sorry, but your son didn't survive."

Later, the trooper would hand deliver his written report to us, detailing the wreck. Chris's truck broke down, and he got a ride, unknowingly with a drunk driver. The driver was traveling more than 100 miles per hour when the car flipped over three times, throwing Chris over 350 feet from the vehicle. Chris sustained a broken neck and numerous other injuries. The drunk driver walked away unharmed.

My legs buckled as the officer's words began to pene-trate my denial, and I felt my husband's strong arms catch me from behind as I cried, "No, God, not Chris!"

I dropped to the floor and curled into a fetal position. With my head tucked in, knees tightly packed against my chest, I whispered, "Please, God, I need You. If You're there, God . . . can we talk?" Then blackness closed in.

There, near the front door, I slipped into another world. Still curled into a fetal position on the floor, I entered into a heavenly dream and saw myself with Chris in heaven. How indescribably wonderful that was! But all too soon I stood in front of God, feeling defenseless and spiritually naked. I could feel God searching my heart, my mind, and my soul.

"Jan, why did you turn your back to Me all these years?"

His question cut straight to my heart. "I thought You didn't love me anymore, God. After all the sexual, physical, and emotional child abuse, I felt too soiled, too dirty, too unworthy to pray, or even think about reading my Bible. And then I made my life worse with alcohol, sex, drugs, and cigarettes."

"I was still with you, waiting for you to call Me for help."

I closed my mouth, silent, expecting to hear God tell me how disappointed He was with me. Instead He said, "I love you, and I have always loved you. Even when you walked two steps from the gates of hell, I loved you. Understand this, My daughter. I love you even though you have sinned."

Awakening from that trance-like dream, tears of sorrow, grief, and regret flooded my face, and I could feel the warmth of God's strength encompass my entire being. My body felt numb, weightless—as if administered a massive dose of Novocain.

And then the doorbell rang.

"Honey," Bill said softly, "Pastor Nelson is here."

"What? Who?" I sat up slowly. Then I remembered.

Chris had broken and trained a couple of Roger Nelson's Appaloosa colts, and Roger was the minister of Lone Jack Baptist Church where Chris was baptized.

Roger and Bill helped me to the kitchen table, and then Roger held my trembling hands and prayed softly. "Dear God, help Bill and Jan during this tragic crisis. Encompass them with love and compassionate support."

By mid-afternoon neighbors and members of Roger's congregation, people I had never met, knocked on my door to express their sympathies. They delivered baked hams, casseroles, and homemade pies. Others brought freshly picked flowers from their gardens and placed them on the lower steps of my front porch. Just before sundown, I glanced out the kitchen window toward the south barn and noticed two young men in my barn, feeding the horses and cleaning their stalls.

I was stunned by the kindness of those who didn't even know me. They simply came because they knew and loved my son, and they expected nothing in return.

Somehow we got through the next few days of

Chris's funeral service and out-of-town guests. Then our home became silent. I wandered around Chris's room, touching his horse show trophies, saddle, and favorite boots. I embraced his pillow, smelling his scent, wishing this were a bad dream and not reality.

Some days I couldn't get out of bed. I couldn't sleep or eat. The heaviness of depression consumed me. I felt as though I was at the bottom of a cold, dark, deep well with no way to climb out. I watched the world in slow motion, my voice muted and my heart shattered.

I tried to pray, to talk to God, though I didn't really know what to say. Sometimes I talked to Him about my broken heart. Sometimes I talked about my wonderful son, Chris. Sometimes all I could do was groan and cry. I continued to feel that God held me tenderly in His arms and listened to my sorrow.

Several days after Chris's funeral service, Pastor Nelson came by our home again. Sitting between us on our living room couch, he asked, "Would you folks allow me to pray for you?"

Bill and I looked at each other, nodded, and bowed our heads.

"Father, you know the pain of losing a child," Roger prayed. "Your Son was killed, not by a drunk driver but by men filled with hate and rage. God, only You can comfort Jan as she mourns the loss of her only child."

As Roger prayed, I felt God's strength surround me,

and for the first time I realized that God really did understand exactly what I was going through. He had lost His only Son too.

Several months later, shortly before Christmas, Bill and I felt strong enough to walk through the doors of Roger's church, the same church where, at the age of ten, Chris had been baptized. As we made our way up the aisle, people we didn't know walked up to us with hugs and kind words.

"I loved Chris, too," said an elderly lady.

"I miss Chris and pray for you every day," whispered a young boy.

"May we sit beside you today?" asked a middle-aged couple.

We were humbled by the kindness and love of this warm church family, these people who loved Chris and also loved God.

The service began with Roger's comments about the beautiful Christmas tree located next to the piano. "Some of you may have noticed our new Christmas tree in the front of the church. Our church purchased this reusable tree in honor and memory of Chris."

I glanced at the wooden cross on top of the tree and silently prayed, "God, thank You for helping us." God had heard my desperate cries. He had reminded me of His love for me, and He had continued to love me and listen to me as I poured out my heart to Him about my son.

When Lightning Struck

HELEN GLISSMEYER

I don't have a zigzag haircut anymore. Nor do I have any scars from the lightning that struck me several summers ago in Daniel, Wyoming. But I still have a deep conviction that my grandfather's prayer brought about a miracle.

I remember the dark sky and the distant lightning flashes as I worked on my grandfather's ranch that August afternoon when I was seventeen. I had just brought in my last truckload of baled hay from the wide open fields. I knew it was going to rain, but it never crossed my mind that the storm would threaten my life. I just wanted to get as much work done as I could before the rain came.

I parked my semi behind another hay-filled truck driven there by my younger cousin, Ross Varner. Then I hurried into the barn. There I helped Ross and my grandfather, Ron Wagstaff, hoist the bales into place with a huge hay fork on a backhoe tractor.

After a few minutes Grandpa asked me to go out to the cattle feeder, which was about a hundred feet away, and clean out the strings. These are plastic ties which are taken off the bales and left in the feeder. They need to be cleaned out before spring so the animals can use the feeder before the grass grows high enough to graze on. The bars on the feeder were metal, a perfect target for lightning. But I didn't think about that until it was too late.

While I cleaned up the strings, Ross and Grandpa worked fast to get the hay unloaded before the rain came and the lightning grew worse. We all knew that storms come up quickly there in that area, and after what had happened in the past, we usually headed for cover anytime we saw lightning.

Lightning had killed a white horse that Grandpa had given to me about two years before. It also hit a big barn that was full of hay and expensive tools. The barn burned to the ground.

We thought of this that day as we unloaded the hay and heard a few faraway rumbles of thunder. Then suddenly we heard a loud roar of thunder that was really close. It spooked Ross and Grandpa, and they decided we all should go in. They looked around for me and couldn't see me.

Grandpa said, (they told me later) "She's probably already gone back to the house."

Then they jumped into Grandpa's little Honda and started for the ranch house, which was about a city block away. As they pulled out, they saw something startling. Two boots were sticking up from a pile of dirt. They looked at each other and shouted, "D.J.!"

Quickly they drove to where I lay, fearing the worst. There I lay unconscious. They told me later that most of my shirt was gone and a zigzag mark on my bare chest looked as though it had been drawn with a black marker. My baseball cap lay several feet away.

Together Ross and Grandpa lifted my limp six-foot frame into the Honda as quickly as they could. Ross said, "It was pretty scary." Grandpa says he dropped Ross off at the house and told him to call the nearest clinic, which was in Pinedale, and tell the medical people there that he was bringing me in.

After Ross called the clinic, he called my home in Salt Lake City, Utah, to tell my mom and dad, and also my grandma about my accident. He later related that he was "so nervous I could scarcely talk."

On the way to the clinic I gained consciousness, and as I woke up in the back of the car, I was confused and didn't know what was happening. I felt numb. I couldn't move.

"What happened? Where are we going?" I asked. My grandpa kept patting me and saying that I was going to be all right.

At the clinic, medical personnel put me on a gurney. They cut my shredded shirt from my body, and they stuffed cotton into my bleeding ear. They put me in a restraint that clamped around my body in case I had neck and back injuries. Apparently the lightning had knocked me a few feet.

The doctor at Pinedale suggested that an ambulance transport me to a larger clinic in Rock Springs for further treatment. By the time I arrived in Rock Springs, my parents, Douglas and Jennifer Holland, were there to meet me. I was so glad to see them.

When the emergency room physician examined me, he found that my right ear was severly burned. Much of my hair above the ear had melted off, and my face was scarred with burns. Fingerlike projections all down my body resembled burst capillaries. The physician told my parents that he was amazed that I had survived the lightning strike.

"I'm going to arrange to have him taken to the University of Utah Medical Center burn unit in Salt Lake City," he said.

During the ninety-minute ride to the Salt Lake hospital, I was awake and aware of the trip. Then in my room a few hours later, a crowd of my worried family members had gathered. By now it was the middle of the night.

My parents and four sisters and my grandparents were there. Ross and other cousins and aunts and uncles were there. Suddenly the room became quiet, and my grandpa said he was going to offer a special prayer for me.

Grandpa asked the Lord to bless me that I would completely recover from the accident, and that I would have no scars or ill effects. After his prayer, I had no doubt that I would be okay.

During my twenty-four-hour stay in the hospital, I learned that besides the extensive burns on my body, my eardrum was seriously damaged. I learned later that sometimes the eardrum will rupture because of the loud percussion of thunder. But, after Grandpa's prayer, I didn't worry about that.

I soon realized I needed to do something about my hair. When the barber saw me with half my hair burned off, and heard about my tangle with the lightning, he said, "I know just the haircut for you." Then he shaved the rest of my hair, except for a zigzag, lightning bolt strip down the center.

During the next few weeks I returned to the hospital several times to have my burns checked. They were healing. Then I went with my parents to an ear specialist. He told us that the burned-out eardrum probably wouldn't mend, and that he might have to graft in a new one. Only time would tell.

Just two weeks after the first visit with the ear specialist, I went back. This time the doctor was really surprised. He found that my eardrum was actually growing back. It wasn't completely healed yet, but it was growing back. It was a hope-filled miracle!

Now several years have passed since I was struck by that bolt of lightning. There are no signs of the scars on my face or body. All my hair grew back some time ago. I have no hearing loss. I even have to stop to think which ear received the damage.

I still have a strong conviction about hope and the power of prayer. I had said a lot of prayers back then after the accident, and so had my family. But I know my grandpa's prayer in the hospital was the most powerful one of all. It was the one that brought about the miracle.

The Real Miracle

CANDY WOOD LINDLEY

By the time we pulled up to the hospital entrance that Tuesday in May 1982, the afternoon sky was nearly as dark as midnight. The wind whipped the trees into a near frenzy, and the rain was coming down in sheets, as thunder rolled and lightning zigzagged across the heavens. Despite my forced optimistic demeanor, the weather matched my mood, and I was having a hard time maintaining my usual sunny disposition.

Of course, I really had no choice. I wasn't about to let anyone know how absolutely terrified I felt as I climbed out of my mom's car and turned back to say good-bye. Known by some as Miss Dramatica, I was playing one of the toughest parts imaginable.

As I watched the yellow Camaro pull out of sight, I tried to ignore the growing sense of loneliness that threatened to overwhelm me. *No,* I thought. *I can't let this get the best of me.* And so I turned and pushed my way through the rotating doors and walked across the lobby to the admissions desk.

After smiling my way through the admissions process, I was sent to radiology for a tomogram of my head.

"What's a tomogram?" I asked the technician, almost forgetting to smile as I listened to his matter-of-fact answer.

"It's just a fancy x-ray," he said. But I wasn't satisfied.

"Does it use much radiation?"

"No, not at all," he assured me, and then proceeded to situate me on the cold metal table and strap down my head before telling me to be still.

"Don't move your head," he said—as if I could—and then he left to go into a control room.

When he finally returned, I asked, "Why did it take so long?"

Without looking directly at me, he explained that tomograms take longer than x-rays.

"What did you see?" I pressed, my heart beating faster by the minute.

"I just take them; a radiologist has to read them." His smile was quick and impersonal. "You can get up now," he said, removing the strap from my head.

I soon found myself in a hospital bed, propped up on pillows and gazing out the window at the Birmingham skyline, hidden now by a bleak, black blanket of clouds. The May thunderstorm that obliterated the skyline was nothing compared to the storm of emotion that was about to break loose inside me. Now that I was by myself and no longer felt the need to perform, a sick feeling ran through my stomach.

Before long, my husband, Lee, arrived. The two of us were watching television when one of my surgeons came in.

"You don't look very cheerful," I said, trying to keep my tone light, even though somewhere deep inside I already knew why he wasn't smiling. "Have you had a bad day?"

Dr. Goldfarb turned to me, his words as somber as the expression on his face. "After looking over your tomogram, it seems the growth is larger than we thought."

I was right, though I hadn't wanted to be. The doctor's previous assurances that it was just a pea-sized growth that needed to come out faded to the back of my mind. Still, I did my best to ignore the implication of his statement by quickly responding, "So you take out a larger growth."

He began to explain to me about a tumor "the size of a golf ball in your sinus cavity," but I cut him off.

"Just get to the bottom line," I said. "What's the worst that could happen to me?"

Without hesitation, he looked me directly in the eyes and replied, "You could lose the right side of your face."

Stunned, I asked the next question, one I had asked before but now felt compelled to ask again. "Why? It couldn't be cancer, could it?"

Compassionately, yet again without hesitation, he answered, "Yes, Candy, it could. But remember, you asked for the worst. Let's just hope for the best."

My greatest fears, those I had tried to bury for so long, were finally beginning to surface. And there was nothing I could do about it.

From the beginning of this ordeal, I had chosen to believe that I or someone else could fix things. After all, I was an only child, and I had always been able to depend on the art of persuasion or just plain stubborn persistence to get what I wanted or needed. Why should this be any different? And yet I knew it was. In fact, I knew there was a very real possibility that I would not live to raise my two young children.

We quickly called my parents and two of our pastors to come and pray with us, but by the time everyone went home that night, leaving me alone in my room, I had no more answers and no more peace than I had before they'd arrived.

I spent a sleepless night waiting for the surgery that was scheduled for 7:30 Wednesday morning, a simple procedure that amounted to cutting across the top of the teeth under the lip on the right side and removing the tumor from the sinus area. By the time I was wheeled into surgery that morning, I was starving for words of hope and reassurance.

Dr. Goldfarb was the last person I saw before I was

put to sleep. Mary, his nurse, held my hand in both of hers, as Dr. Goldfarb and the other surgeon, Dr. Poyner, stood beside the operating table. Pleading with my eyes as well as my words, I looked at Dr. Goldfarb and, as if I could change the circumstances by begging, said, "Doctor, what do you think?"

In an obvious attempt to encourage me, he repeated his words from the night before: "Let's just hope for the best." But his half-smile and the concern in his deep brown eyes gave him away.

Back in my room a few hours later, I heard Dr. Goldfarb's voice, penetrating the lingering haze of my anesthesia.

"The mass was larger than we had anticipated—the size of a baseball. We didn't try to remove it; we just took a small section to biopsy. The frozen section has the correct characteristics of being malignant, but the pathologists aren't sure."

My mom's voice asked, "When will they know?"

"Possibly tonight," the doctor answered, "but probably tomorrow."

After drifting in and out of pain for the rest of the day, I still had no answer. By Wednesday evening, I was silently praying and begging the Lord to hurry things up, to let me know the biopsy results, whatever they were. But somewhere, deep in my soul, I already knew.

"Momma," I said, as the truth of what lay ahead permeated my thoughts in a way I didn't understand and couldn't explain, "I'm going to go through something so horrible that people won't believe it, but it's going to be okay in the end. I'm not going to die." When my mother responded with a puzzled look, I added, "I wanted to say it out loud so when it happens, people will know I didn't make it up."

It was a statement that was to border on the prophetic in the months and even years to come.

By the time Dr. Gerwin, Dr. Goldfarb's and Dr. Poyner's partner, came into my room to check on me late the next day, I hit him with questions the moment he walked through the door.

"Do you know anything yet?" I asked, almost before he had a chance to introduce himself.

"About what?" he asked.

"About the biopsy report," I answered anxiously.

He shook his head. "I don't see an official report in your chart yet."

"So they still don't know whether it's malignant or not?" My frustration was tinged with relief; there was still a ray of hope.

Dr. Gerwin's brows drew together. "Well, I don't think there's any question about that," he said.

My heart began to race as I went into my denial mode. "Dr. Goldfarb says there's a possibility that it isn't," I argued. Actually, no one really knew, but when I had asked Dr. Goldfarb if there was a possibility it wouldn't be cancer, he said yes. I guess I took that the way I wanted to, but Dr. Gerwin's next statement hit me hard.

"I certainly would never go so far as to tell you that," he said, and then changed the subject, informing me he was going to remove the packing from my nose.

Now I'd had packing before—a square gauze pad rolled up that easily slid out of the nostril—and that's what I expected would happen this time. I wasn't at all prepared for what was about to occur.

Taking hold of the protruding tip of gauze with his instrument, he pulled inches of the bloody packing out of my right nostril, along with what felt like my entire nasal membrane. It took my breath away and brought tears to my eyes. When he took hold again, I squeezed my eyes shut.

"No! There can't be more," I insisted. But there was.

As he ripped out another section and the tears began to stream down my face, my pitiful whimpers turned into pleading.

"Please. Please don't take out anymore," I cried. When I realized he was indeed going to take more, I bargained for time. "Please. Wait. Let me get my breath. May I have a sip of Coke?"

"Sure," he agreed. As if he had nothing else to do, he waited patiently for me to calm down. "Whenever you're ready."

After my little break, I told him to go ahead. With every muscle in my body tensed, I closed my eyes, held my breath, and clutched the sides of the bed. He pulled one more section.

"How much more is left?" I was crying by then but trying hard to hold it in.

One more section ripped through, and then another section—seventy-two inches in all. By the time that last inch of gauze was removed from my nose, I was exhausted and weak.

After he left the room, I couldn't contain my emotions any longer. Turning my swollen, aching face into the pillow, I began to sob, uncontrollably and long into the night, until it seemed I had no more tears to cry.

And then I lay there in the quiet. Now what? Physically drained from the ordeal earlier, beaten down mentally and emotionally, my thoughts turned back to God. I had prayed to receive Jesus Christ as my Savior when I was fifteen, but like so many other things in my life, I simply checked it off my list of things to do. I had never even read the Bible, except as an assignment for a class in college, where it was treated as a historical account. I sometimes went weeks without thinking to pray. I tried hard to be moral and good, and Lee and I were both involved in our church. I worked with the church's camp for underprivileged children, Lee and I had taught junior high Sunday school, and I was president of the ladies' organization the year before. But spiritually I was obviously missing something.

"Lord, I am so sorry. I realize now that I need You—for everything. I don't want to deal with this. I don't want to make any more decisions. You're going to have to do it for me. I don't even know how You do that. But whether I live or die, I'm totally Yours to do with whatever You want." And I meant it. I surrendered everything—my hopes, my dreams, my desires, and my very life to the Lord. It took being at the very end of Candy—emotionally, mentally, physically, and spiritually—to begin with God.

And so I was changed forever, though I really didn't understand that at the time.

As it turned out, the biopsy showed that I did indeed have bone cancer, resulting in the need for six surgeries over a three-year period, leaving me facially disfigured. Though I didn't lose the right side of my face, I came close. My face is crooked now; I wear a hairpiece to cover a couple of large, permanent skin grafts, and bangs to cover my sunken-in forehead, where the doctors were unable to replace the bone above my eyebrows. My marriage to Lee eventually dissolved under the pressure and he filed for divorce, and I went through physical and emotional challenges and upheavals that I never would have imagined I could survive, just as I declared to my mother that I would. But also as I declared to her, I did not die. In fact, the pathologist at the Mayo Clinic called me one of his "miraculous cures." I am alive today, serving God and rejoicing in the way He has restored everything that was stripped away from me, including giving me a wonderful new husband named John.

But the real miracle came when I surrendered everything to the Lord—my health, my family, my future, my life—and allowed Him to completely change my heart. And it was there that I found the miracle of hope and perfect peace that enabled me to move forward . . . whatever tomorrow might bring and whatever the outcome.

The Faces of Hope

JOHN DEVITO

It was 7:40 A.M. that sparkling September day when I unlocked our office on the eighty-seventh floor of Tower One in the World Trade Center. Though it meant getting up at five o'clock in my home about forty miles north in suburban Westchester County, I loved these quiet moments before the frenzy of another day's trading began.

Alone in the office, I could listen to the voice of the great building itself. Ironworkers will tell you that steel sings; to me, whose parents came here from Italy, the sighing of the mighty steel girders was the notes of an opera.

Sure, this Wall Street area, where I'd worked more than half my forty-five years, was a competitive, me-first kind of place. But standing there at the window with a large coffee from my favorite place on Fulton Street, I liked to spend a few moments taking in the beauty. The Statue of Liberty . . . the Hudson River glinting in the sunlight. This was my town. From here I could look down on the rooftops of Brooklyn, where I'd grown up and where my parents still lived. Even when it came time for college I hadn't wanted to go anywhere else—I got my degrees a couple of miles uptown at NYU.

My team at May Davis was starting to arrive. We were a small investment banking firm, raising capital for start-up companies.

"Morning, Harry," I greeted my friend and our head trader, Harry Ramos.

"Morning, Adam, Hong, Dominique, Jason."

Fourteen of us in all, ten men, four women. As the hum of a busy office picked up, I checked my e-mail, glanced through the papers on my desk, reached for the phone to—

The room lurched right. I nearly fell off my chair, then clutched the desk as the room jolted left. An earth-quake? A ceiling tile clattered onto my desk. Light fix-tures dangled, wires spitting. "It's a bomb!" someone yelled.

For a stunned moment we stared at one another. "I'll go check!" I ran into the corridor. Smoke. People peering from office doorways. I groped my way through the haze, past the elevators, down the hall to . . . I stopped.

The rest of the corridor was gone. Where a row of doors had been, I found myself staring down into a hell-hole of fire and twisted steel.

Burning debris cascaded around me. Without think-ing, I snatched a broken piece of wallboard and beat at the flames. It was a moment before sanity returned. I rushed back to my office, where others were doing futile things too: collecting files, packing up big desktop computers. Outside the window where I'd stood sipping coffee, things were falling. Papers, hunks of metal.

Dust and smoke seeped from the ceiling. As chief operating officer I knew I should give some kind of direction, but what? Where to turn? I was a churchgoing man, but at that moment of fear and mounting chaos, God seemed awfully far away. Was my duty to stay and safeguard company property? Strange how slow the mind is to grasp enormity . . .

Adam Mayblum had kept his head and was ripping up his shirt, passing out strips to use as face masks. At last reality got through to me: get your people out of this building. I ran to my desk and called my wife, Marilyn. "I love you, Mar! Tell the girls I love them!"

I grabbed a half-gallon bottle of water, got people to moisten their makeshift masks. Some of the staff still looked undecided. "Joanne! Sam! Everybody! Let's go! Leave everything!"

In the corridor the smoke had grown thicker. "Not the elevators!" I shouted. Pressing the wet cloth over my nose, I led the way . . . right . . . then left . . . Where was the exit sign? I'd passed it a thousand times, scarcely seeing it—who takes stairs from the eighty-seventh floor? We were almost at the chasm where the hallway ended when I saw the sign glowing redly through the gloom. If the floor had fallen in a few yards nearer, there would have been no exit.

The stairwell was filled with acrid smoke and fleeing people. Narrow . . . stay together . . . go single file. "Put your hand on my shoulder," I told Jason. "Everyone hold onto the one in front." The fourteen of us formed a chain and started down. Eighty-sixth floor . . . eighty-fifth . . . Around us people were saying an airplane had struck the tower. It was incomprehensible. Yet there we were, struggling through the smoke, the ordinariness of the day torn asunder.

At the seventy-eighth floor the stairway suddenly ended. Seventy-eight was a transfer floor. The stairway continued somewhere on the other side of an open area around the elevator banks. We stepped into a scene of pandemonium. In the choking dust hundreds of people milled, looking for an exit. From the ceiling exposed wires sent showers of sparks into the crowd. Small fires crept along the floor. There were screams, people crying, people praying.

In the press and the confusion, our human chain broke up. By the time we located the stairs I'd lost track of Harry, Hong, and several others. "Go ahead!" I told the rest, "I'll stay and look for them."

Jason pulled my arm. "John! Don't be foolish. This building's on fire! Think of Marilyn, your girls!"

Maybe the others were ahead of us, maybe they'd found another staircase. We went on. Seventy-third . . . seventy-second. More and more people with every floor, progress so slow. As a terribly burned woman was carried past, I battled the fear clawing inside me. I wondered where God was in all this terror.

After thirty floors my legs were shaking with fatigue. I stopped, passed around the half-gallon bottle. Fifty-fourth . . . fifty-third . . . Almost half an hour and we'd only come this far!

Still fifty floors to go. A stream of water from the automatic sprinklers was making the steps slippery. People stumbled and fell. Others helped them up. I could no longer see anyone from my office. Forty-sixth . . . forty-third . . . forty-first . . .

It was then that I saw him. He was a fireman toiling up the stairs, heavy equipment strapped to his back and sweat streaming down his face. He stopped just below me and tugged off his helmet. Short-cropped blond hair, brilliant blue eyes, the map of Ireland on his face. He was red with exertion—but there was a glow about him I thought was more than that. Why did I feel I ought to know him?

"You look like you need some water," I said, holding out the half-full bottle.

The blue eyes looked into mine. "I'm all right," he told me. "Give it to somebody else."

He put his helmet back on and kept climbing. I went on down. Thirty-eighth floor . . . thirty-sixth. Give it to somebody else. And suddenly I knew whose face I'd seen above that fireman's raincoat.

It was the face of Jesus.

Thirty-fifth floor . . . thirty-fourth. I began to notice something I'd seen without taking it in. In that stairwell jammed with terrified people, there'd been no shoving. Wedged together in a narrow stairway of a burning building, no one pushed ahead of the slow movers. Over and over I'd witnessed just the opposite! The handicapped given precedence. Men stepping aside for women. The young giving place to the gray-haired. As injured and burn victims were carried past, everyone flattened against the wall, called encouragement, waited. Same thing as the firefighters climbed up.

Twenty-ninth floor . . . twenty-eighth. I blinked. That young Asian woman with her arm around a frail older lady—surely it was Jesus who looked out of her eyes! Again . . . I glimpsed Him in the eyes of the Pakistani man motioning me to go first. God far away? God was right here, all around me on that crowded stairway, wherever one person reached out to help another.

Once more the water bottle came back to me. All those hot, hurrying people, but each one took only a sip or a drop to wet a handkerchief. Give it to somebody else. All around me the face of Jesus. In the caring, generous, giving people of a competitive, me-first world.

Three exhausted firemen were on the landing of the fourteenth floor. I left the bottle with them. Tenth floor. Seventh. And suddenly I was outside.

My relief was chilled by the scream of sirens. Fire trucks everywhere. Ambulances. Police shouting, "Move! Keep moving! Don't look up!"

And at that, of course, everyone looked up. A giant plume of black smoke trailed from high in the building. No . . . from both buildings! Our twin tower, Tower Two, also on fire? Around me people were saying two airplanes had hit. Two? But that had to mean . . .

Someone shouted my name; next instant I was embracing three of my team! "Get out of here!" a policeman shouted at us. I looked up.

And saw the impossible. Tower Two was falling. The whole enormous structure thundering down.

A deafening roar, people shrieking. I ran, but the hot black cloud came faster. In seconds I was smothered in a stinking, suffocating blanket of heat and dust. Blinded, stumbling, I could only pray I was running in a straight line and not back toward the collapsing giant. Around me were cries, running feet, but I could see no one. It was darkness as I'd never imagined dark. An organic, breathing, malevolent blackness.

And suddenly I knew what this dark cloud was. Minutes earlier I'd looked into the face of Jesus. Now I was encountering the darkness of evil.

If Jesus was love, this was hate. Tripping, choking,

gasping, knowing now that this destruction was deliberate, I understood that this is what hate always does. Blinds us to one another, spreads its all-obscuring cloud to keep us from seeing one another's faces.

Through squinted eyes, I saw light ahead. The putrid, strangling cloud was thinner. I burst into a store—a record shop—and gulped the sweet cold air. Someone gave me water, urged me to sit, but after calling Marilyn and my parents, I had to keep walking. Heading north . . . anywhere away from that faceless night. Chinatown. The Village. Washington Square Park. Looking at people. Looking at Jesus.

And looking for a church. Any church, where I could tell Him that my life would be forever different. I had always believed in Him; now I'd seen Him.

I caught sight of myself, too, reflected in a store window and understood why some people drew back as I approached. I was blanketed in ash, a gray specter. Others, though, ran toward me. Reached out, grasped my hand, hugged me.

Somehow I'd come all the way to the NYU campus. I went into a church and knelt in a pew. And for the first time, I cried.

Marilyn had told me not to battle the crowds trying to get out of the city; her cousins on Leroy Street were expecting me. I walked there from the church. The Perazzo family rushed down the steps of the brownstone to greet me, let me shower, tried to get me to lie down. But I couldn't stay indoors, couldn't handle walls, a ceiling. All afternoon I sat outside on the stoop, under that bright blue sky, my back to the smoke shrouding the south of my city.

When I learned that Tower One had fallen, too, faces sprang in front of me. The blue-eyed fireman who wanted me to give the water to somebody else. The policeman standing at his post telling others to move away.

And the face of Harry Ramos. Phone calls had located all the rest of our staff. Only later did we learn that trim, athletic Harry had stayed behind on the thirty-sixth floor to help a heavyset stranger who could walk no farther.

Bobby Perazzo couldn't resist telling his neighbors on Leroy Street, "My cousin was there! He was in Tower One!"

The word spread among passersby. A tourist couple from Utah embraced me. A Puerto Rican lady said, *"Vaya con Dios,"* It was Jesus, of course. All of them. In a burning building. On a New York street. Whenever darkness threatens to overwhelm us. Wherever love and hope glow on a human face.

Chapter 3

Hope Comes Softly

No one whose hope is in you [God] will ever be put to shame (Psalm 25:3 NIV).

Sometimes when we sit quietly in the presence of God, hope comes into our lives softly, like gentle butterflies that float in on gossamer wings and perch on our shoulders. As long as we are still and quiet, hope remains with us, content to be in our presence. But when we begin to flail about, fighting with life and drowning out the soft voice of God with our own shouting, hope may suddenly fly away. Be still. Be quiet. Watch and listen for the hope of God that comes softly.

A Glimmer of Hope

NANCY B. GIBBS

I need a little glimmer of hope, God," I begged. The prior six months had been hard for me. My best friend had passed away. My husband, son, and grand-daughter had all been hospitalized for critical or unusual illnesses. We were still fighting some of these problems. The doctor told me that my husband had an incurable heart disease. That didn't make me feel any better.

My daughter had been involved in a minor car accident. She wasn't hurt but her car had to be replaced. I had several physical problems of my own. Earlier that week the doctor informed me that I needed to have surgery.

While sitting in my recliner feeling as low as I have ever felt in my life, I made my request to God. I felt the urge to go outside even though the air was cold. We had had several cold days that week.

The trees were barren, the grass was brown, and the world seemed lifeless—much the way I felt. When I closed the back door behind me, my dogs became excited to see me. I went to their section of the yard, opened the gate and went inside to play with them. A few minutes later, I saw my glimmer of hope. In the corner of the yard was a single daffodil. It was perfect. The bright yellow flower instantly warmed my heart. I knew right away that it was God's answer to my prayer.

With tears falling from my eyes, I picked the flower. I took it inside, placed it in a bud vase and admired it for several days. If that little flower could make it during that cold, windy day, surely I could endure the storms in my life too. All I needed was a little glimmer of hope.

Hot Potato, Cold Potato

B. J. TAYLOR

I hate you!" I yelled, as I ran up the stairs to my room. Throwing open my dresser drawers, I pulled out a clean T-shirt and jeans, threw them in my backpack, and ran back down the steps. Mom and Dad stood there in shock.

"Where are you going?" Mom asked.

"Anywhere but here," I shouted as I ran out the door. They weren't fast enough to grab me, and I slipped away into the night. It was cold, but my hot temper warmed me, and I didn't feel it. Not at first anyway.

I hit the streets with my thumb out. Hitchhiking wasn't safe, but I didn't care. It was the only way I knew, at fourteen years old, to get away from them. We'd moved three times in the last four years. I was always playing catch-up at school and trying to fit in.

Worse than trying to fit in was trying to make new friends. There were cliques of popular students who had known each other since grade school. Then there were the geeks and jocks who just didn't seem to interest me. I wasn't athletic and didn't excel at anything really. Just an average high school kid looking for friends. Deep down inside I knew my parents loved me, just as God loved me, but it wasn't enough.

I slept curled up on a park bench the first night I took off. It was hard as a rock, and I was surprised to find that I wasn't alone. With my arms wrapped tightly around me for warmth, I huddled on the bench closest to the streetlight. Peeking through half-closed eyes, I could see other homeless people just like me, only they looked like they'd been there a long, long time. Some of them looked kind of scary, with dirty beards and baggy clothes. Some pushed grocery carts filled with their entire life's treasure. I didn't sleep much that night, and when the sun rose, I washed up in the park's restroom and hit the road.

By the end of the second day, I'd made my way to another city sixty-five miles away where I found a halfway house for runaways. I was tired, cold, and hungry. By the time I got there, the kitchen was closed. All that was left on the table was a cold potato. I lifted it to my lips and bit into the wrinkled skin. It was crumbly and dry, and stuck in my throat when I tried to swallow. That night I slept on a cot in a room with four other runaways. It wasn't a whole lot better than the park. The cot was hard and the blanket was scratchy, and those other kids looked like they'd been there a long, long time. I tossed and turned all night.

The next day I changed into the only clean clothes I

had and was shown how to use the washer and dryer to do my own laundry.

"The soap is over there," Carly told me. She was one of the other four runaways in my room. "Don't use too much, just half a scoop is all you need."

I wanted to ask her how long she'd been there, but she interrupted my thoughts.

"I've been here almost four months now," Carly said. "We have rules for what you can and can't do, so you better get used to it. You can't use the laundry before 8:00 in the morning and you can't watch TV after 10:00 at night. You have to be down at the kitchen table right at 12:00 and 5:00, or you don't eat, and you have to rotate chores every week. This is my week on kitchen duty. I help make lunches and dinners, and I clean up afterward. So don't go makin' a big mess in there."

"When are you going home?" I asked her.

"I don't know and I don't care. My parents know I'm here but won't come by to even talk to me, and so what! You got something to say about that?"

Carly glared at me as she talked.

"No," I responded, but I felt sad for Carly. Her parents didn't even care! I was scared. Maybe my parents didn't care, either.

Three days later, my dad showed up at the front door of the halfway house. I don't know how he found out I was there, but part of me was glad he did, though I wouldn't admit it out loud. After gathering my few things, we drove home in silence. I could almost see the questions running through his head. *Why did she run away from home? What was so awful there that we couldn't talk about it?* I could see by the look on his face that he felt responsible for all my anger and sadness. I regretted shouting at my parents the night I ran away. It wasn't their fault that I felt this way.

I had a long time to think as we drove those many miles home, and I wondered why I hadn't seen all the things Dad had done for the family. He was trying to make a better life for us, moving us from one city to the next so he could get a better job. He was doing his best to clothe us and feed us. It was up to me to make the best of a new school and to open up to new classmates. Sulking around in the halls and not taking part in social activities wouldn't help me make friends. Maybe I could make more of an effort to reach out to others.

When we finally reached our house, Mom opened the front door as we walked up the stairs. I smelled a roast cooking and knew there'd be hot baked potatoes to go with it. As I stepped inside, she opened her arms wide and I fell into them. Dad was right behind me and put his arms around both of us. Ordinarily, I'd pull away, but this time I didn't.

They both released me a few moments later, and that's when I saw the tears in Mom's eyes. I lowered my head and blinked twice really fast, trying to hide my own tears. I made a promise to myself not to hurt them like that again.

Years later, when I was a grownup working hard to make ends meet for my own children, I trusted in the optimism I grew into as a teenager. I had wished for a better relationship with my mom and dad and eventually I had one. I had hoped for a different family and a different life way back when I was so young, but I had the best family and best role models a teenager could ever have. It just took me some growing up to realize it. My hope had come true.

The Perfect Grandchild

NANCY JULIEN KOPP

D ad couldn't deal with handicapped individuals. He changed the subject when a special-needs child became the topic of conversation. *If you don't talk about it, you don't need to recognize children born less than perfect.* He never voiced it, but his actions and attitude spoke volumes.

Ironically, I taught a class that included several handicapped children. Maybe his attitude is what made me so bent on helping these children. My dad didn't want to hear about them when I came home to visit. He abruptly changed the subject whenever I tried to tell a story about one of them. I hoped he'd see that they were no different than any other child. They laughed, they cried, they wished for special things, and they had likes and dislikes.

When our first baby arrived shortly before Thanksgiving of 1966, our anticipation and joy turned to shock, for Julie was a spina bifida baby. Along with silver blonde hair, big blue eyes, and skin that shone like satin, she had an open spine and paralysis of her legs, bowel, and bladder. My husband relayed the sad news to both sets of grandparents. The message we received from three of them showed nothing less than hope and acceptance. My dad had nothing to say about his first granddaughter. He visited me in the hospital and pledged his support and love to me for rough times ahead. Sadly, his visit didn't include a peek into the nursery.

Within days, Julie became a patient of a well-known neurosurgeon at a children's hospital in Chicago. He closed the opening in her spine and inserted a shunt to drain fluid from her brain. It was so much to endure by one tiny soul. I wasn't able to stay with Julie, as a difficult delivery, a slow recuperation, and distance kept me at home where I agonized over our separation and spent a great deal of time in prayer.

My mother and I spent our phone calls talking about Julie. I tried to live with hope, but sometimes hope is a fragile entity. Mom's positive words buoyed me up when I occasionally fell into despair. I spoke to the nurses daily, and we went to visit our little girl every weekend. To us she was perfection.

One night during the second week, my dad called. "I went to see Julie today," he blurted before even saying hello. My heart skipped a beat, and I clenched the phone. Dad went on to describe all he'd seen at the hospital, how impressed he'd been, and how beautiful Julie looked. His voice quivered more than once as he talked to me. Tears flowed down my face at the knowledge that my dad was beginning to accept a handicapped grandchild. I knew how hard that visit had been for him.

It was the first of many such visits. Dad worked several blocks from the hospital, and he spent many of his lunch hours walking through the cold, rain, or snow to check on Julie's progress. His reports to me were descriptive and filled with love for both his daughter and granddaughter. I could detect a little more acceptance on his part with each visit to her. One evening he called, and I noted excitement and pleasure in his voice as he told in great detail of seeing Julie receive a Christmas doll from a hospital auxiliary volunteer. The woman tied the tiny doll to Julie's isolette within her line of vision while Dad watched. He described the doll from head to toe as well as the red satin ribbon used to fasten it. They were words I needed to hear since I had not been present, words I came to treasure.

Dad's visits came to an end in the middle of January when Julie died. Despite our grief, I gave thanks that my dad had come to accept a less-than-perfect child as part of our family. Her time here was limited, but she taught Dad a lasting lesson, and the bond between my dad and me grew stronger than it had ever been. A loving God performed a miracle using a tiny soul, who worked her way into her grandfather's heart, one short visit at a time.

Christopher's Gift

ALEXANDRA LIGHT AND S. A. FOREST

Christopher was the black sheep of his very traditional, meat-and-potatoes, sports-oriented, middle-class family. He grew up in a section of Brooklyn where young men were supposed to be tough. But Christopher never fit in—not in his family or his neighborhood. Sensitive, creative, Christopher made it apparent, even when he was very young (much to his family's dismay), that he was different from the other children.

"Chrissy the sissy," as the other kids called him, was interested in the arts—and that just didn't go down well in his part of Brooklyn. Things got worse when the other kids found out he was taking dancing lessons, and worse still when it was rumored that he was gay. His father was particularly hard on him, and his two older brothers and sister were not much kinder. But being the youngest, he always was favored by his mother. She didn't understand him either, just loved him unquestioningly, and Christopher felt very close to her.

When he was sixteen, Christopher moved out and found a place to share and a job in Manhattan. All of his free time was devoted to studying dance. At eighteen he was accepted into the *corps de ballet* of a prominent dance company. At twenty he switched to modern dance and was hired as one of the principal dancers in an up-and-coming company. Everyone said he had a promising career. But when he was twenty-three, he injured his knee and had to stop dancing. Two years later he moved to San Francisco.

From the time Christopher left home until he moved to San Francisco, he had made weekly visits to his mother, slipping in and out when the others were away. He hated the long subway ride to Brooklyn, and his old neighborhood depressed him, but he was a dutiful son and rarely missed a visit. Three years after he left home his father died; in the years that followed, the other children left home one by one. By the time he moved to San Francisco, his mother was living alone.

Now, whenever he went home, Christopher noticed that his old neighborhood was dramatically deteriorating. On each of his visits, Christopher would try to get his mother to move—as did his brothers and sisters—but she wouldn't hear of it. This was her home. This was where she had raised her children. She had a wonderful park practically outside her door. She knew all of the shopkeepers—although a great many had closed their stores and moved on. All her friends were there—

although their ranks were thinning. Christopher was a very persuasive person, but nothing could get his mother to change her mind. She just wouldn't budge.

One day, Christopher got a phone call from his sister. He'd had little contact with his siblings, and from the urgency in her voice he immediately knew that something was wrong. His sister was beside herself. The neighborhood had taken a dramatic turn for the worse. Junkies had moved in. One of his mother's neighbors had been mugged and had to be hospitalized, and another had her apartment broken into. His mother's apartment building was being neglected and vandalized. The buzzer system and the lock on the front door were broken. His sister was truly afraid for their mother's life, but she didn't know what to do.

By now Christopher's mother was over eighty years old. She could barely hear, even with a hearing aid. But she was still a very independent, active person. She wouldn't dream of moving in with one of her children, and wouldn't even consider a nursing home. His sister had taken her to different facilities, and the only place their mother would agree to move to was a senior citizens' residence in Westchester, an upscale area about an hour from New York City. She'd fallen in love with the place the moment she saw it. The grounds were lovely, the staff friendly and caring. It was a short drive to her daughter's home, but she would have her own apartment and wouldn't have to give up her independence. She was ready to move in on the spot.

Unfortunately, space was limited, and there was a long waiting list: two years, one at the very least. Given the unsafe conditions in their mother's neighborhood, his sister was afraid she wouldn't last the year. But their mother would just not hear of moving anyplace else, even on a temporary basis.

When Christopher got the call he knew he had to fly to New York immediately. He didn't know what he was going to do; he just knew he had to go.

All during the flight he kept asking for guidance: "Please, God, tell me what to do." When he stepped off the plane, he had the answer, but it didn't make any sense. He'd been told to gather everyone in the family together at his mother's home. He didn't see how that would help or change anything, but over the years he had begun to trust in His guidance.

Now, Christopher's brothers and sister barely spoke to one another, and there was so much bad blood between his aunts and uncles and cousins and nieces and nephews that getting them all together under the same roof seemed as impossible as bringing peace to the Middle East. Not only that, they were scattered all over the country. But Christopher was determined. By hook or by crook he managed to get each and every one of them to come to his mother's house in a week's time. He didn't tell anyone what it was about. All he would say was that it was a healing, a matter of life or death, and if they came they would witness a miracle. By noon the following Sunday, sixty-three anxious, hostile members of his family—many of whom he hadn't seen since he was a child—were packed into his mother's living room.

When Christopher stood up and silenced everyone, he had no idea what he was going to say or do. For the first few minutes, his mind was a total blank. He could feel himself begin to panic.

While he was waiting for inspiration, he just looked at everyone. Many of these people had been less than kind to him. But instead of harboring ill feelings, he felt his heart fill with love and compassion. He realized that their lives had not been easy. Suddenly he knew what to say.

First Christopher spoke about what a loving person his mother was, how she never said a bad word about anyone, how despite the family feuds, each and every one of them had always been welcome in her home, how at any hour, night or day, there was always a full plate of food for anyone who dropped by.

Then he outlined the problem. He emphasized that he wasn't asking for solutions. No, that wasn't what this gathering was about. Christopher was a firm believer in the power of love, and he was asking everyone to put their differences and grievances aside, and join together to use the collective power of love to create a miracle. It didn't matter if they didn't believe in it, if they thought it was all a bunch of nonsense, all they had to do was get in touch with a warm feeling and open their hearts.

To help them, he asked anyone who wanted to to come up and talk about a loving experience they'd had with his mother. One after another, more than half of those in attendance got up and recounted a story. Even more would have spoken, but there were so many, and it was getting so late in the day that Christopher finally called a halt to the sharing.

All during this time, even though she couldn't hear what anyone was saying, his mother had an incredible glow in her eyes. She might not have been able to make out the words, but she was getting the loving feelings that were being conveyed.

Before Christopher ended the healing with a silent prayer, he told everyone that they were the miracle they had come to witness. Their willingness to come to his mother's aid was a sign of the love in their hearts, and this love, their love, was the miracle. He said it was clear, from the loving looks on their faces, that the hatred and anger they'd brought with them had drained from their hearts. He said he'd always known that, if they put aside their differences, they would simply love one another. That love was the reality, and conflict and separation the illusion. Christopher was as surprised as anyone by what he was saying.

When the prayer was over, relatives who hadn't spoken in thirty years were hugging and embracing and kissing one another. Children who normally taunted each other were playing peacefully together. There was hardly a dry eye in the room.

Still, Christopher couldn't see what good he had done. Sure, peace had been restored in the family, if only for the afternoon. But how was that going to get his mother out of her apartment? By the time he boarded the plane back to San Francisco the next day, he was ready to write the whole thing off as a waste of time.

Two weeks later his sister called to tell him that his mother had been accepted into the Westchester facility. She didn't understand how, but a space had opened up, and his mother's name had leapfrogged to the top of the list.

Christopher's mother lived there for the next ten years. Each time Christopher visited or spoke to her on the phone, she told him that these were the happiest years of her life.

During his last visit she took Christopher aside and told him that even if nobody acknowledged it, she knew he was the one who was really responsible for getting her off the waiting list and into the residence. She called him "My miracle worker." Two months later, on her ninety-first birthday, she died peacefully in her sleep.

Walking Miracle

CHRISTY LOWMAN

I t was a beautiful summer evening in August. My mother, brother Jeremy, husband, and I decided to go out to eat. We decided on a buffet-style restaurant because the thought of homemade, honey-butter rolls made my mouth water.

"Mom wants us all to ride together," I said to my husband.

"Nah. We'll just meet them there. We need to go to the grocery store afterward," he said.

"Okay, I'll let her know," I said.

We followed them to the restaurant and got there around 9:00 P.M. We enjoyed each other's company just as much as the delicious meal. I sampled almost everything; I ate so much I had to undo the top button of my pants!

We said our good-byes on the way out the door. They headed back home, and our trip to the store turned out to be a waste of time, because it was closing as we pulled into the parking lot.

On our way back, we came up on a line of traffic

about a mile from my parents' house. A terrible feeling came over me.

"It looks like a pretty bad accident up ahead," my husband said.

"Donnie, it's Mom and Jeremy," I said.

"No, it's not; they're probably already home," he said.

"No, I know it's them. I've got a terrible feeling that it's them. My stomach just started hurting really bad too." I said, doubling over in pain.

"We'll turn around and go the long way around to your mother's, so you'll know they're fine," he said backing our red truck in the ditch to get out.

As we pulled into their driveway we noticed their car was not there and the house was pitch dark. As soon as my husband shut off the truck, a huge wave of pain overwhelmed me, and I became sick to my stomach.

"I've got to use the bathroom, and while I'm in there I'll call Dad and tell him I think they have been in an accident," I told Donnie.

I called my dad at work and was told he had left for an emergency. I knew my gut feeling was right, but I kept hoping for the best.

We went back to where the wreck had occurred. There was still several vehicles and ambulances there.

"Christy, whatever you do, you stay here. I'll go and see if it's your mother and brother," Donnie said.

I nodded my head in agreement as I tried to keep

my food down and my increasing stomach pain under control.

It seemed like eternity before he came back to the dirt parking lot where I stood. By the look on his face, I could tell he was struggling with what to say. "Your brother has been sent to Valdese Hospital and your mother is on her way to Baptist Hospital in Winston." His words struck me like a hammer, knocking the wind out of me. I struggled to keep my reeling mind on what he was saying. "We will go and see your brother first and then your mother," he said. He added almost in tears himself: "They were hit head on by a drunk driver going seventy miles per hour. He died instantly." I collapsed sobbing when I heard the rest, staggering back to the truck, certain I would be sick.

After the sting set in, my stomach eased off somewhat and I prayed the entire way to the hospital where my brother was taken. I also prayed for the man's family in the other car, hoping that Jesus would be meeting him soon.

On the way, my husband sighed heavily and said in a low and unusually serious voice, "I lied to you, but I had to," he said looking at me with a sad look.

"About what?" I asked

"Your mother . . . your mother is still there. They are still trying to cut her out of the car. Your father is there, too, standing beside her. I lied to you because you did not need to see it. You would have made things worse and would have been in the way. Besides, your brother needs you more right now. I'm sorry, but your dad and I thought it was best." For a minute, we sat in silence, and I didn't know exactly how to feel. I felt glad that my husband spared me from a scene that would have most certainly haunted me the rest of my life. At the same time, I was furious that they thought I was unable to handle such a situation, and I really wanted to see Mom. Just as I was about to erupt and lash out in pain and anger, my husband, I think sensing my growing anger, locked eyes with me and asked, "Do you forgive me?" All at once I realized he was doing his best in an incredibly horrible situation.

"Yes, I understand why you said it," I said looking down at the floorboard. Then with a dirty smirk he added, "The good part is there's not a single hair on her head out of place."

"Well" I said stunned. "She would not have liked that. You know how particular she is about her hair."

Instantly, we both burst into a nervous cackle as he came to a stop in front of the emergency room.

I don't know why it struck us so funny, or why he felt pressed to say it right then, but I thanked God for that small amount of light He brought to us in such a dark time.

We had arrived at the hospital at the same time they

were trying to insert a catheter in my brother, and having him drink the orange contrast stuff for X-rays. Our youth pastor was there, but shot out of the room like a gunshot when the orange contrast was spewed. Hoping there was enough of it still in him, they proceeded with the X-rays. After a few minutes the doctor came out and informed us that my brother was very fortunate, he just had some cuts and bruises, but they still wanted to keep him overnight for observations. My aunt volunteered to stay with him while we left for the hour-and-a-half trip to the hospital where my mom had been flown.

We arrived there around 2 A.M. to find my dad and the pastor sitting in the waiting room.

"Mom's in surgery. It's going to take about eight hours," Dad told me. "Then she will have to undergo several more. She has several broken bones and her foot is crushed and almost amputated. They are working to save her foot now. Her hip, arm, and collarbone are all broken too, but she will be okay. The doctors said it's a miracle that she's alive."

The pastor prayed and stayed with us that night. The next morning I finally got to see Mom. As I came in, I realized how hard it was to see her this way. Groggy and confused from pain medication, she kept asking what was wrong with her, and what had happened. She could not remember anything that had happened. The bags of blood from the numerous blood transfusions were a constant reminder of her hour-and-a-half wait to be removed from her car. The doctors were convinced she would never walk again.

A few weeks went by and the surgeries were completed with more to come in the next few months. During this time she never once became bitter at God or asked Him why this had happened to her, and never became angry at the situation.

"I *will* walk again," she insisted over and over, even though her chances were very slim.

I, on the other hand, wondered why it had happened; my mother was a godly mother. I was thankful that she was alive, and I knew there was a reason it happened, but why to such a godly person? She was also a part of numerous outreach programs for God and that would now be put to a halt. What would she do? I also blamed myself for picking the place to eat that night.

Mom stayed in the hospital for about a month and then was put in a rest home close to the hospital for physical therapy for another two months. We traveled the nearly two-hour drive almost daily for the entire time she was there.

The rest home was hard on her. The nurses wanted to treat her like the others there. Tried to make her wear diapers at night and didn't want to help her much. She was treated as a burden when she needed to brush her teeth, take a bath, or use the bathroom. They also would leave her food by the door on the other side of the room from where she was lying bedridden. A lot of times she had to manage on her own or forget it, hoping for someone to help her the next day.

Her first roommate had Alzheimer's disease, and during the night tried to pull the devices that were screwed into her leg off. God assigned a caring nurse and she made sure Mom was taken care of. Then He sent a new roommate, who helped her tremendously.

"I don't know why this has happened, but I know God has a reason for it, and it will be used to glorify Him. One day I will walk again," she would always say to me hopefully when I came to visit her with a smile on her face. There were several times we thought she was going to lose her foot, but I think her hope in God and her determination is what got her through it. Today Mom walks! It has been seven years now and she still has to go to therapy several times a week, but she walks! She has a wobble, but her doctors are now saying that one day she may even walk without a limp. She has a plate and screws in her arm and foot and has gone through two new hips, but hopefully there will be no more surgeries.

She is truly a walking miracle!

A Bigger Plan

CHARLIE W. SHEDD

This is a story of one of my failures. By my standards, it was a failure, but God had a bigger plan. That's how it often is in His prevenience—love ahead of time.

For my text that Sunday, I had chosen Joel 2:25: "I will restore unto you the years which the locust hath eaten." Not much background in the passage, really. However, I did like it, and wasn't "like it" where my elderly mentor had told me to start? Yet somehow, though I honestly tried, it simply wouldn't preach. For me, the poor thing fell with a dull thud.

I could tell that even Martha had her doubts. When we sat down to her customary Sabbath spread, things were not like our Sunday noon custom. Her usual "I think you're wonderful" smile was a bit subdued. So we discussed my feelings and her feelings. Then we decided together we should put this week's feeble effort out of its misery. We did. With a special prayer for that kind of misery, we laid it away.

Only it wouldn't stay away. All afternoon it would

push over the tombstone and leer at me. Fortunately, it was a busy Sunday and busyness is good balm for sore memories. But there is another balm I like. On my way home I decided a thick Barmore milkshake was exactly what I needed. I call this "Comfort me with something creamy."

Fred Barmore was one of our elders. Good man. Good friend. He must have recognized the downward thrust of my spirits, so he made the shake that Sunday exactly like I loved his shakes—extra size, extra sweet, extra thick. Delicious. Super soothing.

Halfway through this sin of the flesh, Fred remembered something. Suddenly he got up from the table where we sat visiting and ran to the cash register.

"There was a couple in church this morning from Ogalalla. Nice folks. They stopped here for a sandwich. And when they left, they gave me this envelope to give you first time I saw you."

If I were to list on five fingers the most beautiful letter ever to come my way, this one would surely be included:

Dear Reverend Shedd:

We are from Ogalalla and on our way to Lincoln. Since we always go to church, we stopped today for your service.

There is no way we could tell you what your sermon meant to us. Actually, we were heading for Lincoln to consult a lawyer friend. Sorry to say we were going to work out details for a divorce. We had both decided our marriage was hopeless.

But here we sit in this drugstore having lunch, and as we waited for our order something happened we think you should know. We began discussing those simple little rules you gave for restoring a marriage the locust had been chewing on so long. The more we talked the more we knew the Lord had been speaking to us through you, so this is what we decided to do. Instead of heading for Lincoln, we're heading back home to begin restoring what was once a wonderful love. Thank you.

Why did they happen to be going through our town at everybody's church hour? Did they feel the brush of an angel's wing guiding them our way? Ours is the God who rescues failures. By angel or whatever the method. That's exactly what He promised in the morning text, isn't it? It's a great promise.

> *I will restore to you the years*
> *that the locust hath eaten.*
> Joel 2:25 KJV

The Last Visitor

MODESTE SLYWKA

Visiting hours were over. It was almost 11 P.M. on Thursday, January 7, the Feast of the Three Magi. My physician, who had left his office to admit me into the hospital, was gone. And the priest who had just given me the Holy Eucharist was getting on the elevator.

I was praying for comfort and strength. I had orbital cellulitis. A flesh-eating bacteria that had invaded my sinuses and ate its way into my left eye socket was now threatening my eye, brain, and life. The left side of my face was swollen to distortion and the hospital staff was concerned that I would not live till daybreak. Tears were rolling down my face. I experienced profound dread.

Then I heard, "Hi!" An extremely thin, beautiful teenage girl was standing in my room, holding on to an IV stand with a tube running into her nostril. I had never seen anyone so thin. She came closer and gave me an ever-so-faint smile.

The next thing I knew, a nurse was waking me up to draw blood and change my IV bags (five). It was day-break. The nurse, Maryanne, told me that the swelling of my face had stabilized and all three antibiotics and steroids were starting to take effect. I had survived the night.

Beautiful Jennifer and I spent the next two days together while I waited for the swelling to subside to the degree that they could operate and try to save my eye. I found out that she was in the hospital for the second time in a year for starvation. Jennifer spent much time telling me that there was no tangible reason for her to eat. That nothing really mattered. Living was a drag. That no one really cared. That the initial hunger pangs left after several days, and then eating became irrelevant. Her existence became a vacuum. This brought me to a state of sadness and tears, for she was the angel the Creator sent to me in my darkest hour.

When asked by her, why the grief? I told her that I understood her rationale for not eating. She seemed genuinely surprised by this. I went on to tell her that many years before, when I had been abusing drugs, I would not eat for a week at a time. Eating had not made any sense. You just forget about it. And after all, it had seemed to me at the time that no one really cared. So why should I have cared about living?

Jennifer asked me what changed me. I told her that I met some people who helped me find my Creator. They told me they had faith in me, that I was born innocent, fell into darkness, and could work my way back to innocence. God loved me. Everyone had a reason for living. We just have to live to find it.

Jennifer asked questions. I answered them as best I could. She began to draw pictures as we talked, primarily of her perception of angels. I told her she was gifted, that if she died no one would ever see these beautiful drawings. She smiled.

Saturday at around 5 P.M., my doctor told me it was crucial to operate immediately. The swelling in my face had subsided to an acceptable risk factor, permitting surgery. As I was praying, Jennifer came into my room and gave me a drawing of one hand holding another. It was titled "Helping Hand." Peace came over me, and I entered the operating room that way.

After almost four hours of surgery, they saved my eye. Back in my room after post-op, Maryanne, my nurse, came in to check on me. Seeing me awake, she told me that Jennifer ate a whole meal for supper that night. I smiled even though my face hurt.

During the three days prior to being discharged, Jennifer and I started to laugh a lot, about everything; it didn't matter what. We were goofy. She began finishing every meal. Her father visited her. We all said hi to one another.

In being the vehicle of hope to me, Jennifer, I believe, found a reason for living. How dark it is before the dawn.

It was time for me to leave. I stopped by Jennifer's room on the way out; we were only two rooms apart. She was on the floor, drawing a very large portrait of an angel. She looked up and gave me that beautiful smile, although sad. I told her that if it ever gets dark for her, to think of me and say "Hi." That I will be with her always.

The Mysterious Stranger

DONNA GOULD

After my daughter Sara turned thirteen, nothing seemed to work in her life. She was failing miserably in school and absolutely nothing we did for her helped. She was depressed, unhappy, and generally feeling horrible about herself. When she turned fourteen, things got even worse. My husband and I were called to the school more times than I can count, and we were always told that she should be left back a grade. Basically, all her teachers had given up on Sara. Her personal life as well as her school life declined considerably. Not only was Sara failing in school, but she was being teased daily, and her friends turned away from her. Finally, we were at the end of our rope.

A good friend suggested that we send her to the local Catholic high school. I called the school and was told bluntly, "The entrance test was already given and there is absolutely no way that she can get in." I begged the school to at least take my name and number, and if something opened up to please call me. The administrator repeated her negative response in a voice I will never forget, "There's no chance at all of your daughter getting in this year, sorry!" With those words, we sank even lower. Every day I saw my daughter's mood change and the sadness on her face deepening. We needed help desperately.

Three months later, I got a call from the "new school." The same person who told me that there was not a chance at all now said, "If you're still interested in having your daughter take the entrance test, please have her come in next week." When I told my daughter, her eyes lit up with happiness. Hope sprang again in our life for a new beginning; the hope of wiping the slate clean. But that next week, after she took the entrance exam, Sara walked out with sadness in her eyes. "Mommy, I tried, but the test was very hard and I don't think I did very well." Still, I encouraged her to wait and see, to have a little faith.

The school said they would have the test results in a few days, and when they called, we were informed that Sara had scored above average and that she was being accepted. She was overjoyed. Unfortunately, she didn't pass the eighth grade and was being left back, so we had to turn down the new school's offer to attend.

Then, days later, her current school administrator called and said that if Sara was able to complete a course successfully during the summer, she would in fact be promoted to the next grade. I immediately called the new school, hoping we could still take them up on their offer, but since the school was closed for summer, there was no answer. Nonetheless, I ran upstairs to get my daughter and said, "There was no answer at the school, but let's go there and see if anyone's in." I didn't want to give up. Yet when we arrived, all the doors were locked, not a single person was to be found. The school looked like a ghost town—no noise, no people, nothing except silence. My daughter and I looked at each other and knew that the opportunity to attend the new school had been lost forever.

Suddenly, a man with a beard appeared out of nowhere. He turned to us and asked, "Can I help you?" "Yes," I said. "We are looking for the administrator." He asked why.

I said, "We need to find her. My daughter was accepted and we had to turn down the offer, but now we would like them to reinstate it. Can you get us to her office?"

He said, "Everyone is gone for the summer. Her office is locked, but I'll let you in and you can leave her a note." He looked at my daughter and said, "This is really a nice school. Do you want to go here?"

My daugher looked back at him and said, "Very much. But it's too late. And we turned them down once, so they won't offer us a second chance."

He said, "You never know. God works in strange ways."

After we finished writing the note, we left it on the administrator's desk. The man with the beard turned to us and said, "You have to believe, and you have to have faith." We walked out of the office and turned around to thank him, but the man was gone. It was like he'd vanished into thin air.

The next day we got a call from the school and were told that my daughter could attend after all. Somehow the administrator got the message that we left, even though the school was closed.

Now my daughter's grades are in the 90s. She is happy and well adjusted. Some things in life just can't be explained, and I think this is one of those times. To this day, we don't know exactly how her school acceptance was made possible, but it has made a huge difference in our lives. It's especially made a believer out of my daughter and taught her about keeping the faith even when she feels hopeless.

It may sound very strange because I am Jewish, but we don't know who the mysterious bearded man was that helped us the morning that we went to the school building, and I think he looked exactly like Jesus. Every day I had prayed for my daughter, and I think my prayers were answered.

CHAPTER 4

Surprised by Hope

We have this hope as an anchor for the soul, firm and secure (Hebrews 6:19 NIV).

The events of our daily lives are filled with surprises from God. He keeps us from getting bored with predictability; He prods us out of our ruts and routines; He adds splashes of joy and delight to make life interesting and worth living. When we're facing important, perhaps life-changing decisions, He often surprises us with glimpses of Himself—glimpses of the hope of glory. And that gives us the courage to go forward, staying in step with His plans for our lives. Stay alert! You may be surprised by hope.

The Banner of Love

NANCY B. GIBBS

I n his early sixties, my father's personality changed for the worse. We had gradually noticed many changes since he retired at fifty-five. He had big plans for his retirement years that never worked out. His temper raged and paranoia plagued him. Daddy lashed out at everyone, except me. Suddenly, our family members discovered that I was the only one who could do anything with him.

Therefore, on a sorrowful Sunday afternoon, I was the one who was forced to admit him to the hospital. At the same time, the doctors would try to find a way to stop the progression of Parkinson's disease. When I left him there that day, I sobbed the entire way home.

Until that day, I never realized how badly a broken heart could hurt. We discovered that the medication for his illness caused both the paranoia and the violent episodes he experienced. But when the medication was discontinued the Parkinson's disease progressed rapidly.

A few weeks later, our family had to make the decision to admit Daddy to a nursing home. He needed round-the-clock medical care. My heart hurt even worse that night than the day I took him to the hospital. This all seemed so final.

I cried myself to sleep that night. I woke up the next morning feeling that I had let Daddy down. The doctors had all told me there was nothing I could do to help him. I hated leaving him in that nursing home, however. And I wanted desperately for him to know that I loved him. How would I convince him of my love after leaving him in such a cold and dreary place?

I printed a banner with a cupid at each end holding a scroll. On the scroll I printed these words, "I Love You!!!" I took it to the nursing home, showed it to Daddy, and asked him to read it. I hung it on the wall so he could see it from his bed.

"When you are here alone Daddy and wonder if anybody loves you, just read this banner and remember how much I love you," I said. Daddy smiled and said he would.

For four long years the sign hung in Daddy's room. During that time, Daddy forgot who I was, even though I visited several times each week. He knew he loved me, however, and one day he even asked me to marry him. I smiled and accepted.

Many times I have wondered how many lonely times Daddy read the poster that I made for him. I hoped and prayed that he knew the words were true.

Finally, one February morning, God took Daddy

home. He escaped his frail body and shattered mind. He was made whole in heaven that day. But my grieving heart was shattered. I needed to hold him. I wanted to dance with him. But mostly, I wanted him to say, "I love you!" just one more time.

That afternoon I walked into the empty nursing home room to pack up his few belongings. I took the sign off the wall, carefully folded it up, and took it home with me. I hung it on the wall of my study.

During a difficult time a few weeks later, I fell asleep in the chair facing the sign. I awoke in the middle of the night and the first vision I saw was the banner of love that I had made some four years earlier. The light from the other room illuminated the words that brought me the same kind of hope that I prayed it had brought Daddy. I knew in my heart that at that moment Daddy was telling me that he loved me too.

A Yard-Sale Prayer

KATHRYN LAY

I t had been one of the worst few weeks of our family's life.

Three weeks earlier I had woken up in the night with my leg swollen double, red and purple and painful. I spent eight days in the hospital with a serious blood clot. The stress on my family was enormous. I was depressed and discouraged, asking God over and over why I was going through this time.

Less than a week after I got home, my husband complained of a pain behind his ear, a numbness in his face, a horrid taste in his mouth. Within a couple of days, we knew he had Bell's palsy, something he had had twenty years earlier on the other side of his face. It wasn't deadly, but uncomfortable and frustrating for a teacher who talked all day. This disease could last weeks or months before suddenly getting better.

Three days later, our refrigerator quit working. After nine days dealing with our insurance company and repairmen, it was decided the refrigerator wasn't repairable. More days went by living out of an ice chest waiting for the insurance to approve a replacement. I spent every day trying to get resolutions from customer service and shopping for food day by day.

By the next Friday evening, I was emotionally exhausted and spiritually struggling.

"Are you still there, God?" I questioned over and over.

I told my husband I needed a break from stress and was going yard-sale shopping the next morning.

I got up early, sat in my car with a cup of coffee and prayed. *Lord, I know it's no big deal, but I need something special this morning. I need a little treat, something to make me smile, something that shows me You're still here.*

It seemed silly, praying for yard-sale shopping, but I needed something that morning. Even a small miracle.

After driving around for an hour and seeing only six sales where I stopped at only two with nothing interesting to purchase, I felt even more discouraged. I rarely had the extra money or time to do this and had hoped for an exciting morning rummaging through possible treasures.

I stopped at one yard sale and bought a couple of small things, then left and got lost in the twists and turns of an unfamiliar neighborhood. I was near tears when I finally found the main road and knew how to get home.

"That's it, I'm going home," I said through gritted teeth.

My prayer wasn't going to be answered.

As I left the street, I had to turn the opposite direction from home to make a U-turn at the next crossover. There was a sign at the next street though telling of a moving sale.

"Okay, I'll go to one more, *then* I go home," I said.

The sale was crowded and I parked several houses down. As I walked up to the yard, the first thing I saw was a loveseat sitting near the curb.

It was green. Our living room was green and brown tones in paint and furniture. The loveseat was the same green as part of the stripes on my couch. The same green as the two throw pillows I bought recently.

We'd been wanting a loveseat for a while, more room for when friends came over instead of dragging in dining room chairs.

I sat on the loveseat. It was comfortable. It was in great shape. It was only $100.

The homeowner walked over to me and smiled. "Looks like you need a loveseat."

I jumped up. I *never* bought large items at a yard sale, never without discussing such things with my husband. He was home, still sleeping.

"Uh, well, it does match my stuff. I'm not sure though."

He said, "We're moving to France tomorrow. What would you give for it?"

I hesitated, not good at bargaining. "Would you take $75?"

"Sure," he said.

I had almost hoped he wouldn't. I suddenly felt committed.

"I have a problem though. It won't fit in my van and I don't have access to a truck today."

He pointed to an older man. "That's okay. My father is here with his truck and we'll follow you home and deliver it."

I really felt trapped then. I told him I'd go to the nearest ATM and come back with the money. At the store, I almost got back in my car and drove home.

But it all seemed perfect.

I went back, paid the man and waited while his father got his keys.

"So you're moving to France?"

"Yes," he said. "I'm going to get some training, then teach."

"Oh," I said, "My husband teaches ESL."

He nodded. "That's what I'll be doing. In Africa."

They followed me home and brought the couch into the house. It looked beautiful with everything else.

My teenage daughter came into the room and I introduced them and told her they were moving to Africa. He said, "We're moving there forever." I looked at him a moment. "Are you going to be missionaries?"

"Yes," he said.

I told him that our associate pastor had grown up as a missionary kid in Africa and that my daughter loved hearing his stories. He asked the name of my church and I told him.

His eyes got wide. "Is that Don Barker you're talking about?"

I gasped. "Yes, do you know him?"

He said, "I've met him at the missionary meetings in Dallas."

I nodded. My husband had attended some of those.

I told him how our family had gone through a very rough time the last few weeks and how that morning I'd prayed for a special blessing while looking at yard sales. I stared at the loveseat, fitting in so perfectly with our paint, our other furniture, the only wall space left. It was beautiful and I'd had the money to buy it thanks to an unexpected extra amount in my husband's check. I had given up, ready to go home when God took me to one more yard sale. God had even sent me to someone who was willing and able to deliver the loveseat to our home.

And I'd been able to help a missionary raise money he needed.

I was astonished at the depth of the answer to my prayer. To others it might seem trivial, but there were so many perfections in that little purchase that I knew without a doubt God's hand was in it.

My leg was still swollen and in pain at times. My husband's face still partially paralyzed. The broken refrigerator still sitting in our kitchen, waiting for a replacement.

Yet, I felt lighthearted, wanting to dance around the room at the way God had hugged me that day. It wasn't important in the grand scheme of life, but God saw something that would give me joy and show me that He cared for all parts of my life.

I've had many yard-sale surprises over the years, things I knew came from God at a perfect time of need or want. But every time I sit on or look at this loveseat, I see a Father giving me a miraculous and unexpected gift and I know that He is with me always, restoring my hope.

Even when I sit.

The Miracle of
Lansdowne Lane

GREG ASIMAKOUPOULOS

I hadn't even begun my duties as youth pastor and I already was dealing with the stress related to my new call.

Although we have lived in an affluent Chicago suburb the past decade, Wendy and I weren't prepared for the high costs of owning real estate in the Seattle area. Our beautiful home in Naperville would cost three times the amount if it were located on Mercer Island. Nonetheless, we asked the Lord for just the right place as we contemplated our move west.

On two separate occasions Fred Shore (a Realtor assigned to us by the church) patiently chauffered us up and down the island. He was hopeful we'd find something that would tickle our fancy. Both times we flew home to Chicago downcast and discouraged. There were only a handful of homes available in our price range and none of them made our hearts sing.

After returning home that second time, Fred e-mailed

us a listing that wasn't ideal, but at least caused our hearts to start to hum. Realizing time was of the essence, Wendy and I decided to fly out and make an offer. We purchased our tickets and started to pack. Then the night before we were to leave, Fred sent us sad news. The home we'd convinced ourselves could work was no longer on the market. Someone beat us to the punch.

We decided to make the trip anyway. Perhaps the other person's offer would fall through. Perhaps another home with similar features would become available during the two and a half days we'd be in Seattle. But neither scenario proved to be true.

"Where are You, God? If You've really called us to Mercer Island Covenant Church, won't You confirm that call by providing us a home that would meet our needs?" Wendy and I called out to the Lord in desperation, but our questions remained unanswered.

The cloudy weather matched our emotions the entire time. The skies were dark and dreary. Mt. Rainier remained hidden from view. God seemed hidden as well. One more house-hunting trip appeared all for naught. But then in an unexpected flash of insight, the Lord brought to mind a home I'd forgotten about.

On the Sunday afternoon of our candidating weekend, Wendy and I (along with both sets of parents) visited an open house near the church. Although that home wasn't suitable, it wasn't a total waste of time. My dad engaged a man in conversation who was also looking at the home. This gentleman confessed he wasn't looking to buy, but was actually about to sell his mid-island home. He was there to get a feel for how much he could expect to get for his place.

My dad introduced me to Emilio, who in turn gave me the address of his place. Later that day, before preaching at Carpe Diem, Wendy and I drove out near Island Crest Elementary School to see his home. Since we were flying back to Illinois the next day, I asked if we might see the floor plan and look around. Emilio insisted his house wasn't in showable condition and that he wouldn't be putting it on the market for several more weeks. We left Seattle the following day and didn't give that home any further thought.

Well, three weeks had now passed. Since the Lord had brought Emilio to mind, I wondered about the status of his house. Although I didn't have his phone number, I recalled how to get to his home. I left a note on his front door asking him to make contact with me. When he didn't call back, both Wendy and I were disappointed. It was yet another indication our trip had been a total bust.

The following morning while meeting with members of the church staff, my cell phone rang. A woman identified herself as someone who lived in the house where I'd left the note. She was confused. Her home wasn't for sale and she didn't know anyone named Emilio. I thanked her for her kindness alerting me to the fact I'd left the note at the wrong house. In retrospect, I realized just how pivotal her conscientiousness was to what would play out.

Later in the day I drove back to the neighborhood and found the right house a block away. To our delight, Emilio was home. I reminded him of our previous meeting and once again asked if Wendy and I could see his place. He told us if we came back the next morning, he and his wife would show it to us. We reluctantly agreed. It would mean stopping off before heading to the airport to fly home. But we were out of options.

The rest of the day and into the evening our hearts remained heavy. Emilio's home was thirty-five years old and he'd raised five kids in it. Like others we'd seen, it was probably tired, worn, and dated. We imagined the worst. The special trip out had indeed been a bust. Not even a great seafood dinner at Shilshole Bay cheered our slumping spirits. Still we lay in bed that night asking the Lord for the faith to hold out hope.

The next morning we drove to Emilio's place on Lansdowne Lane. He and his wife greeted us warmly. From the moment we walked in their beautiful home, we felt embraced by a sense of God's presence. The rooms were freshly painted and cheery. The floor plan was what we'd been searching for.

In addition to a living room that flowed into a dining room, there was an updated kitchen and a spacious family room. There were four bedrooms plus an office. Compared to some homes we'd seen where there were evidences of new age religion or paganism, this home had Christian art throughout. And if that weren't all, Emilio's timetable for relocating corresponded perfectly with my start-up date at the church. And had that woman never alerted me to the fact I'd left the note at the wrong place, we would have left town without seeing the inside of Emilio's home. It was amazing!

During the course of our tour of the home, Emilio shared with me that he had a doctor's appointment later that day. Recent tests had confirmed he had a serious heart condition. He admitted to being scared. I felt the Holy Spirit prompting me to suggest we pray. When Emilio said he'd appreciate that, we interrupted our inspection of the home and joined hands in a circle of intercession.

As I concluded my prayer, this near-stranger wrapped his arms around me and gave me a hug. I was moved by Emilio's vulnerability, gentleness, and warmth. Continuing to explore his home, I saw those same qualities evident in the ways he'd cared for a home he obviously loved.

For the remainder of our brief visit, Wendy and I were overwhelmed with a sense that we had found the home the Lord had in mind for us all along. As we said good-bye and walked to our car, tears of joy rolled down my cheeks. God had not been missing in action after all. He had simply been testing our will to trust Him.

Five hours later our Southwest Airlines flight took off from SeaTac for Chicago. I looked out the window at the thick gray clouds that had blanketed the city our entire stay. Once we reached six thousand feet the Boeing 737 was above the clouds. The view I had from my seat was breathtaking. Mt. Rainier stood majestically and unmovable above the clouds. The God of hope and miracles was there all along.

A Real Mother

JAN COATES

I never had a real mother. Instead, I lived under the control of a paranoid schizophrenic, alcoholic, prescription drug-addict mother.

She hadn't always been that way. Members of her family told me that Mom was feisty, full of life, and a beauty when she was young. She married Dad during the Great Depression, when she was sixteen. The following year she gave birth to her first child. Shortly after the baby's birth, Mom began to exhibit signs of mental illness.

Her illness worsened as she bore each of her eight children. More than once I watched from the stairway as Dad covered his face with his hands and bawled while an ambulance driver dragged Mom out of our home in a straitjacket. After a two- or three-month stay at the hospital, she returned home, and each time she seemed better—temporarily. But even then she was distant, and her seeming indifference hurt me most because I wanted her to love me. When I tried to get physically close, Mom pushed me away or said, "Get me something to drink." For her, *something* meant booze.

Dad felt guilty, and I felt responsible. I blamed myself when she drank too much, lost control, or screamed that she hated us all and had never wanted children. Mental institutions, tranquilizers, and shock treatments, coupled with drug and alcohol abuse, made her life a living hell and hurt all of us, even though we tried to understand that she was hopelessly trapped by her illness and addictions.

In that situation, even while I was a child, I became the responsible "adult." I folded the laundry. I helped cook dinner and wash the dishes. I was the surrogate mom to my younger brother and two sisters. If they got a bath, it was because I bathed them. They even called me Nanny. I was sure that if I did the right thing she would get well. I constantly begged God for forgiveness and bargained with Him out of my twisted sense of guilt: if only He would make my mother love me, I vowed to quit lying and stealing.

Mom got worse.

God could not or would not hear my desperate cries for help. Everything seemed hopeless, and I soon gave up and quit talking to God.

Mom's worsened condition destroyed our family. After twenty-five years of marriage, Dad divorced Mom and gave her a generous cash settlement that could have provided for her for at least twenty years. She spent the entire sum in less than twelve months. My siblings and

I felt forced to support her and find her a suitable apartment. She often became violent and abusive to her landlords. One building manger locked himself in his own apartment to get away from her. About once a month I had to find her a new place to live and help her move.

I deeply resented doing that: I was the daughter, and yet she acted like the child. Why couldn't she be like other mothers? Why couldn't she be loving and nurturing—or at least kind? Why did I have to be pseudo-mother to a crazy woman?

One cold, rainy night Mom phoned at two in the morning to tell me someone had poured poison into the heat vents of her apartment in an attempt to kill her. I couldn't reason with her.

"I'm dying, and you don't care!" she screamed. "They'll find my body, and it will be your fault!"

Despite the craziness of those words, I gave in. "I'll be over as soon as I can."

By then I was a single parent. I awakened my four-year-old son, Chris, bundled him up, and drove to Mom's apartment, three miles from mine. Standing outside, we heard music and loud laughing from within. I pushed open the door to find both Mom and the maintenance man drunk.

This was the end; I snapped. I wanted her to go away or die—anything to get her out of my life.

I avoided my mother and minimized my efforts to

help her. I had frightening dreams where I slapped her, pushed her away, or knocked her down. Fearful of my own anger and fed up with her ruining my life, I ignored her crazed phone calls. I saw her only on holidays or her birthday. I wanted control of my life. As long as Mom was around, I knew she would always be there to ruin it.

One snowy night, my boss, Mike, was with me as I drove out of a parking garage. "Hey, Jan," he teased. "Ten points if you can hit the bag lady."

Three feet away was a woman bundled in a tattered coat, wearing two brightly colored hats with a scarf draped around her neck and face. Mismatched mittens protected her hands, and she carried two overstuffed black trash bags. When she turned and stared at me with her piercing blue eyes, I died inside. She didn't recognize me, but I certainly knew her.

Cursing silently, I said, *Oh, God! Don't let her see me. Don't let Mike know that bag lady is my mother.*

I laughed at Mike's joke and pressed the accelerator, veering around and past the woman in the tattered coat. I didn't want a second look at her, but guilt consumed me. *She's your mother,* my conscience said. *She may be crazy, but she needs help.*

I dropped Mike off at the office, drove a few blocks, and stopped the car. I couldn't see to drive—the tears flowed too heavily. I screamed at her. I beat my fists against the steering wheel. Memories of the past flowed through my mind. "God, why can't You help her?" I screamed.

After my chest quit heaving and my screams silenced, I realized I couldn't keep her from roaming the streets during a blizzard, but at least I could help her stay warm and fed. I drove to a farm supply store and bought her a pair of insulated black boots and a pair of waterproof ski gloves. Then, at a corner grocery store, pushing the shopping cart up and down the aisles, I started questioning myself. *What am I doing? She'll never eat this. I'm wasting my time and money.* I angrily shoved the cart ahead and almost knocked down a stack of canned chicken. Without much thought, I thrust four cans of chicken into the cart. Milk, eggs, sliced cold cuts, and cheese. I walked by the crackers and paused. If she'd lost her false teeth again, she wouldn't be able to chew the crackers. I plopped two boxes into the cart. *Maybe she'll choke.*

Bread, soup . . . I hated her for being who she was. I hated feeling guilty. I hated doing anything for her. Where was she when I needed a mother?

Weeks earlier I had placed her in a government-subsidized apartment. I went there, and her name was still on the mailbox. Anticipating her violent reaction, I trembled as I knocked on the brown metal door. "It's your daughter. Open up."

Mom opened the door, wearing a toothless grin and

her latest "Goodwill special" outfit—stained dark blue slacks and a man's plaid shirt. "Come in, sweetie," she said. Her voice was soft, a tone I rarely heard before. "I hoped you would visit me."

I hated being in her apartment. The clutter and trash made me want to go home and soak in a hot bath filled with disinfectant.

Holding back tears, I looked around her small three-room home. All the clothing and toiletries I had purchased for her over the years were stuffed in trash bags and stacked on the floor of her living room. She had stale food and junk from the dumpsters stored in other trash bags. Those stinking bags filled most of the room.

"I brought you some goodies," I said, tearing my gaze from the bags. "You may have to move the beer out of the refrigerator to make room for food."

"No beer, Jan. I'm not allowed to drink anymore. It's bad for me."

"No beer? Really?"

She nodded. "I threw out all the drugs too. They were making me sick."

Hundreds of times in the past she had told me she was through with drugs and beer. And she was—for a few hours.

Don't let her get to you. Put up the iron front. "It's OK, Mom. You're over sixty years old, and I'm a grown woman. You don't have to tell me stories."

"I'm not telling you stories," she said. "I have a job. I go to work. I go to Bible study. This summer I'm going to camp. Come with me tonight for dinner. You'll see."

I had heard crazy things from my mother before, but this was the craziest yet. I stared at her for several seconds before I decided to call her bluff. "OK, what time?"

"We need to leave now," she said. "We have to hurry."

She sat down on a chair and tugged on the new snow boots. "Oh, honey, these will be warm." She smiled at me.

I didn't know where the *sweetie* and *honey* were coming from. Those were not words Mom ever used with me. I was sure she was on some sort of drug. She was too nice, maybe even happy.

We got into the car and drove the dark, snowy downtown streets until we arrived outside a weathered building. The sign on the outside read "The Salvation Army."

"I can't wait for all my friends to meet you," she said. "I'm proud of you. You're my daughter." She looped her arm through mine and escorted me into the building.

What is going on here? This was the sanest, calmest conversation I'd had with my mother since I was a child.

Several people stood in the food line with their plastic trays. One dropped out of line to help Mom find a seat. Another brought her a plate piled high with food. They warmly hugged Mom, and she hugged them.

My mother hugs people?

One of the Army's officers sat beside Mom and another across from her. They spoke softly to her and seemed to genuinely care about her. Mom smiled more during the next half hour than I had observed during my entire childhood.

Someone brought me a tray and made a place for me next to Mom, but my stomach was in knots, and I couldn't eat. Throughout dinner Mom hummed "When the Saints Go Marching In." She smiled frequently and laughed several times.

No one said anything when she stuffed her leftover food into the ever-present trash bag.

These people liked my mother—they really liked her. I could hardly take in what was going on in front of me. Several more people hugged her, called her by name, and treated her like a normal human being.

Slowly I began to understand that a transformation had taken place in her life. God had done what dozens of doctors couldn't do: He healed a broken, mentally ill woman with unconditional love, shining through others. For the first time in my life, I saw peace and love in my mother's heart—a peace beyond description and a tender love that I'd always hoped we'd share.

At the table, Mom leaned against me, wrapped her right arm around my shoulder, and pulled me tight. With her left hand, she snatched the dinner rolls off my plate.

I laughed and grinned at her. She still had some crazy traits left.

She smiled and said, "I love you."

My grin vanished, and tears ran down my cheeks. I couldn't speak for several minutes. Mom and I had finally connected at the heart level. I turned from my uneaten food and stared deeply into Mom's eyes and then at her Salvation Army friends. What I couldn't say to those friends then but said only later was this: "When I could no longer love her, you embraced her. Through your love, God answered my spoken and unspoken prayers and set Mom free from her drug and alcohol addictions. You loved her and showered her with God's love, right where she was—craziness and all. Because of you, I found a mother—a real mother. I had given up hope, but the Lord never did."

Life, a Choice

DARLENE FRANKLIN

*T*hank God for a new day and a fresh start. I poured myself a cup of coffee and uncovered the Chinese checkerboard. While I assembled the pieces, I pondered how to spend the day.

March sixteenth. I thought we'd be celebrating Jolene's birthday today. My daughter was born nineteen years ago. *Not this year.* I hadn't heard from her since police had escorted her to a waiting ambulance on the previous evening.

Jolene is mentally ill. Anything outside of her normal routine unravels the cocoon of progress she has made. High school graduation last May triggered her last hospital stay.

My mother flew in to Denver from Maine for "the birthdays." My son Jaran's birthday is March fourteenth. During his spring break, he arrived from Oklahoma City. For the first time since the children were preschoolers, all remaining family members gathered for the celebration. We planned a special joint event for Saturday, between the birthdays. Jaralene Day, we dubbed it, in honor of the two children.

165

Long ago I learned to plan activities with Jolene's needs and preferences in mind. That way we all enjoy special occasions.

For instance, Jolene loves chocolate cake; Jaran likes anything else. Mom created a three-layer masterpiece that combined white cake with chocolate chips and chocolate filling. I contributed by piecing together the broken bottom layer with gobs of frosting. Two rows of gold candles (one, then nine) honored Jolene's nineteen years; two rows of silver (two and three) recognized Jaran.

Was it only yesterday that we shared a moment of laughter when the candles refused to go out?

Following cake and ice cream, Jaran opened his remaining presents. Books, what else for a philosophy major? Jolene's presents reflected her different interests: an adult-sized basketball to stay active and a porcelain doll to add to her collection. The doll reminded us of a character we had seen on a video, so Natty was christened. Contentment flooded my heart in their delight with their gifts.

For dinner, we went to Jolene's favorite restaurant. It offered something for everyone. She ordered her perennial chicken strips; Mom tried a broccoli cheese soup; and I gummed tender fried chicken. (Recent dental surgery left me toothless.) We carried on a spirited discussion about the chances of the contestants on our favorite television show. We're *Survivor* fanatics. The conversation turned serious; each of us shared ways we had grown over the year.

The waitress topped the meal off by bringing out a complimentary dessert. The "piece" looked like a quarter of a round cake—plenty for all. Four-layer chocolate cake with chocolate icing promised everything Jolene could hope for in birthday delights.

Next we went to see a movie. After the sugar overload of lunch, we ignored the snack bar. With Jolene's need for minimal stimulation, we chose an animated feature. She gives me an excuse to see kid movies; this one was more entertaining than most.

We made it home in the early evening and played a game of Chinese checkers. Since I was still recovering from surgery, I retired to bed while the rest of the family continued playing.

Ten minutes later, my mother shook me awake. "Darlene, I'm sorry. We need your help."

Jolene blockaded the kitchen. She wielded a broom handle and threatened to tear a plastic dustpan to pieces. Chinese checkers playing pieces were scattered across the floor.

"She wasn't winning, and she started throwing things around," Mom said. "I didn't know what to do."

With a sigh for another holiday veered off course and with a prayer for nonexistent strength, I took over. When reasoning didn't work, I took Jolene in my arms and held her in my lap. She relaxed, and I knew I had done the right thing. I called 911. Within an hour she was on her way to the hospital.

No one said anything for a minute.

My mother broke the silence. "What a terrible day. I don't think I'll ever play Chinese checkers again." Her teary eyes reflected the shaking I felt inside.

But I was a veteran of Jolene's bad spells.

"No, Mom," I corrected her. "It was a bad ninety minutes. The rest of the day was good."

"You're right!" she said. "Thanks for pointing that out."

With Jolene's illness, I stopped looking for good days and, instead, cherish good hours. I prize minutes when hours are hard to come by. One bad incident (or a series of bad incidents) cannot dictate my days. To thrive as well as survive, to experience the miracle of hope, I choose to make each day special, good and bad.

I remembered Jesus's words from the Sermon on the Mount. "Therefore do not worry about tomorrow, for tomorrow will worry about itself. Each day has enough trouble of its own" (Matthew 6:34, NIV).

A final swallow of coffee trickled down my throat. The last green peg landed in a hole on the checkerboard. *There, that's it.*

"Mom, Jaran. Come over here. Let's play a game." I smiled, welcoming the day. "It's time to make new memories."

And Baby Makes Three

KATHRYN LAY

Richard and I slipped into the crowded room, our hands tightly clasped. We picked up an information packet and application form, then found two seats near the front.

I glanced around the room. *Were these people as nervous as I felt? Had they waited for a child as long as we had?*

After ten years of trying to get pregnant, a devastating false pregnancy, and years of infertility tests and treatments, we were beginning the adoption process. I didn't feel as if it was the end of a struggle, but the beginning of hope.

I had finally given my barrenness to God, along with the pain and regret. *Having* a family was what was important to us, not *how* we became a family.

Over the years we solicited information on many agencies. Our teacher's and writer's income did not meet the requirements of some, and the long years of waiting did not appeal to us. We had already waited so long.

When friends adopted through the Department of Human Services, we knew this was our chance.

There were no guarantees. We would have to attend

ten weeks of parenting classes, fill out extensive paper-work, open our lives to scrutiny, and be flexible in the age and background of the child we would be willing to accept.

Once the orientation was over, our next step was to fill out an application and wait for an invitation to the classes. On March 11, 1991, we began what was to be months of learning, preparing, emotional ups and downs, and times of wondering if we were doing the right thing.

In spite of all that lay ahead, we were excited and full of hope. For the first time in years, I couldn't wait to look around the children's section in department stores. We talked about how things would be so different through the eyes of a child . . . our child.

Our first hurdle was a stack of paperwork the size of a small phonebook. Hours were spent answering ques-tions about our relationship with one another, family background, what we liked and didn't like, and our opin-ions on child-rearing. We learned more about ourselves than we'd ever known.

The weekly classes were two hours of learning about the children of abuse, neglect or abandonment, and about ourselves. Role playing put us in the children's world, in their parents' place, and that of the casework-ers sometimes caught in the middle.

We knew that somewhere a child waited for us, and we prayed for its safety. At times, I felt guilty. I knew that as we hoped there would be a child for us at the end of our classes and home visits, these children were coming from broken homes. Was my desire for a child so strong that I hoped for such a thing, for abuse or neglect to occur? I prayed and listened to God, and came to understand that the sad truth is that there *are* parents unable to properly care for the children God has given them. Through long years of desire and a heart to love and raise a child of our own, God was preparing us to give a home to these who needed a safe and healthy environment.

One by one, we completed the list of projects that we were given. Health and fire inspections were done on our home, our dog's shots were updated, our physicals were done, and we continued our classes.

Sometimes, we were overwhelmed with all the information and the decisions we had to make about the child we would be comfortable in raising. At times, we left the meetings excited. Other times, we were afraid— afraid of the responsibilities of caring for a child that had been mistreated and the emotional trauma that left scars, whether large or small. Even more, I was afraid that for some reason we would be turned down. I continued to pray that God would be preparing the child we were meant to raise, and preparing our hearts to be ready.

After our first home visit, we felt as if we could float around the house. Our caseworker was impressed with our marriage and what had been said about us from our references. When she left, after weeks of feeling "*if* we adopt," it had suddenly become "when."

Before we knew it, the classes were over. We were

anxious for our caseworker to finish our personal inter-
views and complete our paperwork. We hoped for a child
before the summer ended. With Richard off from teaching for three months, it would be a perfect bonding time.

I began preparing the extra room. Because we didn't
know what age we'd get, whether we'd be placed with
a boy or girl, or one or two children, there was little I
could do but paint and clean.

By the first of July, everything had been completed
and we'd been approved. We prepared ourselves for the
most difficult part.

Waiting.

Whenever the phone rang, my heart skipped a beat.
If we were away from home, we called our answering
machine, hoping to hear our caseworker's voice.

But soon summer came to an end and our extra room
was still empty. I spent time in our child's room, praying
for patience and that the wait would soon end. We knew
that if we were not placed with a child before
Thanksgiving, it would not happen until after the New
Year, as DHS did not approve of disrupting children from
their foster homes during holiday time.

By late September, I was beginning to feel the stress
of the extra classes we were attending—classes on dealing with abuse and its repercussions, on discipline and
on raising the adopted child. I grew tired and resentful
that we had to work so hard for a family.

It's not fair, Lord, I prayed. *Couples who have biological children don't have to have their lives scrutinized, or be trained and taught as if they lacked sense.*

The old bitterness over our childlessness crept back in. The impatience made the waiting seem to last forever. I prayed for peace. I prayed that God would show me He was still there and understood my anxiety.

A few days later, I passed a church. Its marquis shone in the night—"Do we mistake God's patience for absence?"

My eyes filled with tears. Yes, I had wondered if God was ignoring our fears. Yet, I knew that His patience is infinite, for He knew the exact time when that child would come, as when another special child came to an anxious couple in Bethlehem. The peace I had prayed for slipped inside and I felt hope once again.

On October 30, we learned that the eighteen-month-old girl we were being approved for had been placed with another family because of racial differences. I cried all weekend. Why had God built up our hopes only to let us down? I trusted His plans, but I didn't understand why so much sorrow and disappointment had to come first.

On Monday, November 4, 1991, at 2:30 P.M. the phone rang.

"Kathy, is there something you've been wanting for Christmas?" Our caseworker asked.

I gripped the phone and whispered, "Yes."

Teasingly she prodded, "And what might that be?"

The words came out in a rush. "A child!"

"Well, I think we have some good news for you."

Suddenly, all the waiting was over. Our 8 ½ month old daughter was waiting for us, so much younger than we'd even dared to hope for.

But God wasn't finished letting us know how much He loved us. When Richard and I were married, we chose the name Michael or Michelle for our first child, meaning "Gift of God" and "Strength of God." Our new daughter's middle name was Michelle, the name her foster parents had called her since she came to them when only a few days old.

I thought about the sign on the church. Our daughter was being prepared for us, born two weeks before our classes began. The months we had waited and fretted, she was being cared for by a loving, Christian family.

As I look at my daughter, now approaching her first birthday, I think of the verse that God had placed in my heart so many years ago: "He makes the barren woman abide in the house as a joyful mother of children. Praise the LORD" (Psalm 113:9 NASB).

When others see Michelle, they speak of how lucky she is to have parents who will love her. But I tell them that *we* are the ones who were blessed.

Wrong Number, Right Answer

JESSIE MCGINNIS JONES

That morning, February 28, 1992, my granddaughter Melissa fixed my hair at the beauty parlor where she works while I caught up on the local news I had missed during my recent hospital stay. On Valentine's Day, after a spell with my heart, I had had a pacemaker put in. I felt good now and I was glad to be away from all those doctors and nurses constantly fussing at me.

My daughter Rita picked me up at 11:30 and ran me back to my trailer. "Mama," she said on the way, "why don't you come over to my place and I'll fix you a sandwich and—"

"No, uh-uh," I interrupted her. "You already do too much for me. Thank you, I'm fine." Rita was always trying to keep an eye on me, especially since my heart spell. I didn't want to be rude, but I thought I could look after myself. I wanted to convince my six kids of that. It had been a battle just to stay in my trailer. Fact is, at age 80, the more independent I felt, the happier I was. I had been strong all my life. If anything serious happened, Carolyn, another daughter, lived right next door to me. I loved my kids, but I didn't understand what they were all so doggone worried about. I would let them know if I needed something.

I said so long to Rita and thanked her again for her offer of lunch and the ride home. "I'll call you later, Mama," she said, pulling her car away. I shrugged and went inside, latching the chain on the door behind me. I wanted to get a little work done around the trailer, but first I had to get out of my blouse; some hair clippings had caught under the collar and were itching like crazy. I sat down on my bed and pulled my left arm out of the sleeve. Then the right. But something was wrong. *My arm is stuck.* I tried again but my right arm wouldn't move. It was just hanging there. I realized with a shock that the whole right side of my body was limp. *My Lord, am I having a stroke?*

I reached for the phone on the table near the bed. I couldn't coordinate my movements. It was the most frightening sensation. I was helpless, alone. Carolyn had her grandson for the day and probably wouldn't check on me, especially the way I had been carrying on lately.

I managed to slide down onto the floor and tried to kick the table to knock the phone over, but my legs thrashed around uselessly. I finally hooked my left foot around one leg of the table. I gave it a jerk and the phone moved a few inches. I jerked again. A few more inches. Still a long way to go. Again. Getting closer. My strength was failing. Just as I got the phone poised to go over the edge of the table, it rang.

Carolyn? Rita? Oh, God, let it be one of the kids! Two rings, three, four . . . I struggled desperately to topple the phone. *Don't let her hang up. Please don't let her hang up.* I let out a weak cry as I made one last lunge for the table and the phone thudded over on the carpet, the receiver landing just inches from my reach.

My trembling left hand crept toward the receiver, closer. At last I held the cool plastic to my ear. "Help," I gasped. "Help me."

There was a silent pause, then a man's voice hesitantly came from the received: "Wha—what?"

"Help! Please, I need help!" I screamed. But this time I heard myself. My words were a horrible, slurred garble. With fear and frustration storming through my head, I tried it again. "Aaarghhar . . ."

"I'm sorry, I can't understand you. Who is this?" the stranger asked.

I clutched the phone like a lifeline. *Please don't hang up. I need you.*

"Are you hurt? Are you sick?"

Yes, yes! my mind screamed. Then he talked to someone on the other end and a woman's voice came on.

"Hello?" she said. "Can we help you?" Again the horrible sounds came out of my mouth and I was so angry I wanted to throw the phone aside, yet I knew these people were my only hope. *God, help them to help me.*

The voices conferred again, then the woman said, "We've dialed the wrong number but you obviously need help. We're going to hang up and call the police . . ."

"Naahrga . . ." *Don't hang up!*

"Listen, please try not to worry. I promise we'll get help for you."

Then the line went dead. I felt tears rolling down my cheeks as I pushed the receiver back into its cradle. A terrible silence fell over my trailer. Was this how I was going to die? All alone, begging strangers for help? How would they ever find me?

In my living room there is a montage of snapshots I've put together over the years in a big, overflowing frame. Two loving husbands, both of whom God called home. My six children and all their children. Weddings. Graduations. Births. I wanted to crawl there now so I would be close to them if my time was at hand. Instead, gasping for breath, I rolled back against the bed and berated myself for being so stubborn and foolhardy. *All they wanted to do was help.*

My thoughts began to swim and swirl. The shrill ringing of the phone snatched me back to reality. Grappling with the receiver, I finally got the mouthpiece close and made a croaking sound. A woman's voice answered back, "This is 911. Thank goodness we reached you! Now I need your help. I'm going to ask you some questions. Make a sound only when I'm right. We're going to start with the kind of house you live in."

She ran through a list of descriptions: Red, blue, yellow. Big, small, ranch, Colonial. *No . . . no, not a house!* I struggled not to cry out in despair. I tried to send the image over the line to her, forcing myself to concentrate. Finally there was a pause. "I know!" she cried. "You live in a trailer!" *Yes!*

We went through the same process of elimination for the part of town I live in, my street, what side of the street. I could hear people in the background rustling through maps and the phone book. Finally came the one question I was waiting to answer. "Are you Mrs. Jones on Mount Pleasant Church Road?"

Thank You, God! Thank You.

In a matter of minutes Carolyn was talking to me through a window while firemen broke open my door. A short time later at the hospital, doctors confirmed that I had indeed suffered a minor stroke. This time I didn't mind them fussing over me so much, and I couldn't have been happier to see all my children and grandchildren fussing over me, too, during the next few days. I bounced right back and was out of the hospital inside of a week.

The couple who had dialed my number, Mike and Paula Pruitt, had called the police after hanging up with me. They had an idea about how they might have mis-dialed, and 911 took it from there, frantically trying combinations of numbers until they got through to me.

Today I'm back to normal and enjoying my independence again, but I'm not as sensitive as I was about my family looking in on me. They're not trying to run my life; they never were. They just love me and want to keep me around for a while. I've set up an intercom system from my trailer to Carolyn's, and everyone has keys to my place.

We all need one another. Kinfolk especially should stick close. Sometimes it might feel like we're stuffed together in one big clan, knocking elbows and knees and pushing for space like the pictures in my frame. But we are held together by love and by a God who can turn a wrong number into a right one.

A Hopeless Case?

PHYLLIS HOBE

Sitting alone in a restaurant, I fumbled to tear open a sugar packet for my cup of tea. "Here, let me help you," the waitress offered, reaching across the table. I mumbled an embarrassed "No, thank you" and thrust my misshapen hands into my lap. I'd rather go without sugar than be treated like an invalid and call even more attention to my gnarled fingers. *And there's nothing I can do,* I thought. *Nothing!* After a couple sips of tea I paid my bill and left.

My distress had started several years earlier, in 1985, when my finger joints began to swell and stiffen. Things I'd done without a thought all my life became more and more difficult: opening a can, turning a key in a lock, buttoning a blouse.

I went to the doctor, though by then I knew what was happening. "Arthritis," he said matter-of-factly. "All we can do is try to control the swelling and make you more comfortable." He didn't say it was incurable. He didn't have to.

He prescribed anti-inflammatories that were anything but comforting, causing nasty side effects that nearly resulted in an ulcer. Other doctors I went to dispensed the same diagnosis along with prescriptions that either didn't help or upset things further.

Arthritis runs in my family, and my mother had struggled with severe arthritis in her fingers for decades. Now, only in my forties, I was given the same dire prognosis. "Eventually your entire hands will stiffen and look like claws," one specialist told me.

The pain worsened. Sometimes my fingers ached and throbbed, other times I felt a stabbing sensation that took my breath away. Nights were the worst; it felt as if a hot needle had been plunged into each finger joint. *I've got a long way to go in life, Lord,* I prayed. *I need something to help me hang in there.*

As time passed, my hands changed shape. The joints swelled, my fingers curved and I couldn't straighten them. I liked to use my hands to communicate—punctuating my conversations with gestures or an encouraging touch. Now I couldn't stand the thought of everyone staring at the grotesque claws my hands were becoming. I tried to hide them. I wore gloves and kept my hands close to my sides, in my pockets or clasped behind my back. I found myself avoiding any actions in public—eating a sandwich, shaking hands, applauding at a concert. I don't know which was worse, the pain or the shame. At home, grasping the leashes as I walked my two dogs was agony. Everything I enjoyed was affected.

Even typing on my computer was becoming unbearable. How would I do my work as a freelance writer and editor and earn a living? I was too young to retire, and in every other way I was very healthy. Would I have to give up my livelihood?

One day I decided to go shopping. I opened the car door and slid in, then held back a cry of pain as I turned the key in the ignition. My hands were getting so stiff that soon I wouldn't be able to hold on to the steering wheel. I live in the country, where there's no public transportation. *God,* I prayed, *You've got to help me. I can't go on like this anymore.*

Bending my fingers around the wheel, I drove to a department store in a mall about forty-five minutes away. The store was having a sale on housewares, and I hoped to find some pots and pans with larger handles that would give me a better grip. In the kitchenware department, I removed my hands from my pockets only to lift some lids and test their weights.

I picked out a pot that seemed manageable, then went to stand in line. I hid my hands under the pot. But as the line moved forward, I unzipped my handbag to take out my charge card.

I sensed immediately that the person behind me was looking at me. Looking at my hands.

I turned slightly. Sure enough, a woman was staring right at my knobby, red knuckles. I glared at her. Yes, I wanted to snap, my hands are ugly. They look terrible. And they're going to look terrible for as long as I live.

As I turned away huffily, the woman asked, "Don't your hands hurt?"

"Yes, they do," I said, surprised at the concern in her tone. I resisted adding, "And what business is it of yours?" Sympathy from a stranger was not what I wanted. Sympathy wasn't going to heal me.

She moved closer and held out her hands. The fingers were beautifully straight. "My hands used to look like yours," she said. "I had horrible arthritis." She flexed her fingers with ease.

I stared at her, dumbstruck. Was she making a joke? But, no, her eyes were too kind. "What . . . what happened?" I stammered.

"I had some joints replaced," she said. "It made all the difference in the world."

I knew people who'd had hip and knee joints replaced, but I had no idea it could be done with fingers!

My mind raced with excitement as I moved to the counter and the cashier rang up my purchase. Waiting until the woman behind me had paid as well, I asked eagerly, "Where did you have your surgery?"

"In Philadelphia," she said. "I had it done at a hand clinic when it was a new procedure. Some doctors still don't know about it. The surgeons weren't sure how long my new joints would last. But they're holding up fine."

"Thank you," I practically shouted. "Oh, thank you!" I took my package and ran. As soon as I got home, I went to the phone. I dialed information in Philadelphia and asked if there were any hospital listings that mentioned hands specifically. When the operator gave me a number, I began to cry with gratitude.

A few days later I sat talking to Dr. Randall Culp, one of the surgeons at The Philadelphia Hand Center. He put x-rays of my hand on a light screen and showed me how arthritis had worn down the cartilage, so the bones were rubbing against each other. The worn-out parts, he explained, could be replaced with plastic joints, and my body would then produce scar tissue to stabilize the joints. "How soon can you do it?" I asked.

A month later, surgery was performed on my right hand. It required only an overnight stay in the hospital. Compared to the pain I had been feeling, the aftermath of the operation was negligible.

Even better than the absence of pain, however, was the prospect of hope, for hopelessness had become the most terrible pain of all. During the next six months I worked with Terri Skirven, an occupational therapist who taught me exercises to get my fingers working properly again. The exercises would make the scar tissue flexible and strong enough to hold the new joints in place. "You must do these every single day," she told me firmly, "or the surgery will have been a waste of time." I did the exercises for several hours every day until, slowly but surely, my fingers became flexible and strong.

A year later, in 1996, I had the operation on my left

hand. Now, although my fingers aren't perfectly straight, they're supple and work wonderfully. And there's no more pain.

Today I carry cards from The Philadelphia Hand Center with me. And when I'm standing in line or eating in a restaurant or simply see someone passing by whose hands are misshapen with knobby knuckles or swollen joints, I speak up. "Don't your hands hurt?" I ask. "My hands used to look like yours." And then I give the person a card from the Hand Center. I don't care if at first they look dismayed, as long as they discover there is help.

Even when a disease or affliction seems hopeless and tempts you to withdraw, remember there is always help—from others who have had similar experiences, from the latest news, from newly developed medical procedures and surgery. Don't ever close yourself off and assume there's nothing to be done. Even if there's nothing to be done today, it doesn't mean there won't be something to be done tomorrow. In God's amazing world there will always be ongoing research, medical breakthroughs, new therapies and information and understanding. More importantly, God also sends people to guide and encourage us, sometimes when we least expect it.

You may have to learn to live with pain, but there's one thing you never have to live without. Hope.

CHAPTER 5

The Hope of Heaven

"I know the plans I have for you," declares the LORD . . . "plans to give you hope and a future" (Jeremiah 29:11 NIV).

As the old Jewish proverb says, "If you want to give God a good laugh, tell Him your plans." That's because God has His own plans for our lives—plans to lead us through the problems of this life by helping us focus on the hope of heaven. When we fix our eyes on Him and the eternal hope we have in Him, we can overcome the world and its worries and cares, day by day. In truth, the only hope we have of surviving this life is God's promise that we have a glorious hope of heaven for all eternity.

The Cross That Came Back

REAR ADMIRAL JEREMIAH A. DENTON JR.
(RETIRED)

It's very easy to despise our adversaries and condemn them all, without exception. Whenever I'm tempted to do that, I remember something that happened years ago when I was a prisoner of war in North Vietnam.

In the fortress-prison where I was confined, the most reliable way we prisoners could communicate was by tapping in code to neighboring cells. Each covert "conversation" ended with a tapped "GBU" (God bless you). But our requests for church services were denied, and every sign of religion was ruthlessly destroyed.

I had a small cross that meant a lot to me. It had been made by a fellow POW out of bamboo strands. Making it had been a great risk for him; getting it to me was a great risk to both of us.

I knew the guards would never let me keep the cross, so I hid it in a propaganda pamphlet, along with a list of other prisoners in the camp. By day, the pamphlet was under my pallet. But at night, I took it out and held the cross in my hand as I prayed. There was great spiritual comfort in it for me.

I'd had the cross several months when I was told that a North Vietnamese work crew was making its way through the camp, cutting down the ventilation openings in each cell by adding bricks. When my turn came, I was ordered outside while a guard made a search of my cell. In a few minutes, I heard his grunt of triumph. He had found the cross.

Coming out, he stood glaring at me as he broke the cross into bits and threw the pieces into an open sewer. I was furious. Helpless. And suddenly hopeless.

The work crew had been standing by, watching, five or six very old Vietnamese men and women, too old for any other kind of work. They were ordered into my cell to do their job. A half hour passed before they came out and I was allowed to return.

Immediately I reached under the pallet and found the pamphlet. The list of prisoners was gone. Still angry, I began tearing the pamphlet apart. Then I felt a bulge among the pages.

There was a cross. A new one, carefully and beautifully woven from the straw strands of a broom. Obviously the work crew had made it. I shuddered at the thought of the punishment they would have suffered had they been caught.

Then I realized something, something that gave me even more spiritual comfort and hope for the future as I prayed with the new cross. Despite the deeds of men that can make enemies out of strangers, the love of God can still reach down and make brothers out of enemies.

Music from Heaven

PEGGY MCKAY

My mother, Lee, glanced at her watch as she hurried into the house. She wanted to savor those few moments of silence before we burst through the front door with stories of our day at school and the reasons for why we should be allowed to watch television before we did our homework. It was a cold, gray New England afternoon. Lee shuddered and longed for the warmth of a fire as she headed toward the kitchen to fix herself a desperately needed cup of coffee.

As my mother entered the kitchen, she was startled by the sound of an unfamiliar voice singing in the music room. She stood still—frozen—unsure whether she should run or confront the intruder. Then she laughed and breathed a sigh of relief, thinking, *Oh, one of the kids must have left the television on.* However, as she turned the corner to enter the music room, she was confronted with an image she would never forget. There beside the piano stood what appeared to be an angel in a long, flowing orange robe, emanating a bright golden light. The angel acknowledged my mother with a smile and continued to sing.

Lee stood speechless and in awe for several moments until fear overwhelmed her and sent her running to the car. She then drove around the neighborhood until her hands stopped shaking. Suddenly her thoughts turned to our arrival home from school. Scenes from many Saturday-afternoon horror films came rushing back to haunt her. What if it wasn't an angel she'd seen, but a psychotic religious fanatic who broke into people's homes? Or what about that movie in which the students of that demented music teacher kept disappearing?

Lee rushed home and frantically searched the house, now like a mother bear ready to protect her young. But she found no trace of anyone having been there. My mother felt a little crazy and decided not to tell anyone about her experience.

At that time I was thirteen years old. Although I had been playing piano for years, I had only recently discovered song writing. A few days after my mother's angelic encounter, I finished writing a new song and ran to get my mother so I could perform it for her. I sang it with all my heart. When I was finished, my mother stood before me, looking stunned and pale. After an uncomfortable moment of silence, she muttered a few words and hurried back to the kitchen.

I was confused by her reaction, but at that time all adults confused me, so I just kept playing. It wasn't until a few years later that she told me her story so that I would finally understand her reaction. You see, the new song I had written was the same song the angel had been singing.

Not a Second to Spare

KASSANDRA GUYMON

U sually I had to be at school by 7:30 A.M. Northridge High School was doing some testing in the lower grades that day, so we seniors got to go in late. Mom offered me a ride when it was time to go. I sat beside her in our van, kicked off my sandals and daydreamed about my future. I'd be graduating from high school in a few months. This summer was going to be the best one yet. I'd leave high school behind and do whatever I wanted. What would I do? Go to college? Turn my job coaching gymnastics into a full-time gig? Or get a job in an office where I could work my way up? And what about marriage, kids? I had plenty of time to figure all that out later. There were millions of things I could do with my life, and whatever I chose I was sure would turn out fine. Maybe I just had spring fever. Or senioritis. Or a little of both.

Mom interrupted my thoughts. "Kassandra, do you see that?" she asked just as we were crossing the railroad tracks. She stopped the van on the other side and pointed out the window. "It looks like a child." Sure enough, I saw a small boy walking by himself. A blue bicycle rested on its kickstand nearby, but there was no one else in sight.

"He looks too young to be out here alone," I said. The road next to the train tracks was pretty busy and the boy was awfully close to it. What if he tried to cross the street and got hurt? "I'll see if I can find his parents." I slipped on my sandals. "He might be afraid if a stranger comes up to him."

I got out of the van, walked to the nearest house and rang the doorbell. "Excuse me," I asked the man who answered. "There's a little boy over there—he looks about five or six—and he's all alone. Do you know his parents?"

"Kassandra!" my mom called. I turned. I couldn't see the boy from where I was standing. Mom was waving frantically at me from the van.

"What?" I called, a little impatient. I went to the edge of the yard to make sure the boy wasn't in the street.

The warning lights on the train tracks flashed red. The wooden arms descended in front of the road, blocking cars from crossing. The rhythmic chug-chug-chug of a train got louder.

"Run!" Mom screamed from the van. The terror in her voice cut through the clear morning air. The train rumbled into view and let out two desperate whistles. A warning: The engineer saw the boy! But he stayed where he was—right in the middle of the tracks. The whistle sounded again. There's no way that train can stop in time! The boy jumped up and down and waved at the engineer.

I took off running. My sandals flopped against my feet as I ran, so I kicked them off. The train sped so fast. How could I hope to beat it running barefoot across gravel? I ran faster. I tried to picture myself reaching the boy and picking him up without stopping, crossing the tracks just before the train hit us.

Stones crunched and flew under my bare feet. The ground shook. *God, let me get to him!* The train was almost on top of him. But so was I! I put my head down and pumped my legs hard. *Keep going forward,* I thought. *Get the boy and keep running across the tracks. Just a few inches more . . .*

I grabbed the boy in my arms. Keep running! But something pushed me. I fell backward, away from the train. I pulled the boy with me onto safe ground. The train barreled past. The noise was deafening. The wheels were so close I could have reached out and touched one. The train was huge. It was going even faster than I'd thought. I never would have made it if I'd kept going across the tracks, I thought. We would have been killed! I clutched the little boy tightly. Did he have any idea of the danger he'd been in?

Once the train was out of sight I stood up. My legs felt like jelly and I shook all over. I took the boy's hand in mine. Mom ran up and hugged me. "Kassandra, I didn't think you were going to make it!" I held on to the boy. He was much younger than I'd thought. Probably only three or four.

A woman ran toward us. Her hair was wet, like she'd just come out of the shower. I let the boy go and he ran quickly over to her. She reached down and picked him up, squeezing him close to her. "Baby!" she cried. "How did you get out of the house?"

I felt an arm around my shoulders. It was Mom. "He'll be okay now," she said. I nodded, still a little in shock.

Mom looked down. "Oh, honey, your feet!" she said. I lifted up one foot to look at the sole. It was embedded with bits of gravel. Mom leaned down and tried to pluck some of it out.

I brushed the gravel away, still staring at the train tracks. I could almost hear the roar of the train, almost feel it rumbling over the ground. *I could have been killed,* I kept thinking.

I didn't go to school. My legs were so shaky I could barely walk. Usually I considered a day off a rare treat. But I missed going to school that day. All the things about it I'd taken for granted suddenly seemed important.

That afternoon Mom and I sat on the couch, going over what had happened. "I ran at top speed," I said. "All I was thinking was that I had to go forward. The closer I got, the faster I ran. With that kind of momentum I shouldn't have been able to stop at all. But not only did I stop short, I fell backward, away from the train. It was almost as if something pushed me."

Mom was quiet for a second. She looked at me with a strange expression. "In the car I asked God to send angels to protect you," she said. "I guess my prayer was answered."

My own guardian angels. That was definitely something to think about. I got ready for bed that night already looking forward to school the next day. I wanted to enjoy every moment in life. Maybe I'd even go see my school guidance counselor to talk about my future. Would I go to college? Get a job? Have a family? Maybe I'll do all three. Whatever I do, God will be watching over me. And with Him watching over me, anything I hope for is possible.

Standing on God's Promise

BENJAMIN S. CARSON, M.D.

The mother and father standing before me in the consulting room would not believe there was no hope for their four-year-old son. They had brought him to Johns Hopkins from their home in Georgia, where he had been diagnosed as having a malignant tumor of the brain stem, that knoblike cluster on top of the spine through which all brain impulses flow. The little blond boy was paralyzed, comatose; his blue eyes gyrated sightlessly.

I suffered with the parents. I had three small sons of my own. Yet I had studied the x-rays revealing the dark, ugly mass and discussed them with the radiologists and others on the staff. "I'm so very sorry, Mr. and Mrs. Pylant," I said, "but there is no way in which we can encourage you."

The mother's chin quivered. "That's what they told us in Georgia, Doctor, but the Lord led us to bring Christopher to Baltimore because He made it plain there was a doctor here who could help him. We believe you are that doctor."

"But I . . ."

"It's not in the mind of the Lord to let our little boy die, Doctor," broke in the father, nervously twisting the brim of his fedora. "Will you please operate?"

In the face of such faith what could one say?

"I'll do my best," was all I could reply.

The next morning after my regular Scripture reading, I prayed, asking God to guide my hands and mind in the complicated operation facing me. In communing with Him, I thought about all the unbelievable things He had wrought in my life since I was growing up in Detroit's inner city.

My mind drifted back to those days when my mother raised my older brother, Curtis, and me all by herself. She worked hard at three jobs at once, housekeeping in other peoples' homes, caring for their children.

She prayed every day for Curtis and me, and weekly took us with her to church. I loved the stories about the prophets and Jesus and His healings. And when I heard how the mission doctors helped people in far-off lands, I vowed right then and there to become a physician.

I told my mother about my dream as we walked home along the glass-strewn sidewalks one night. Aware of the hopeless-looking men standing in doorways and the squad car racing up the street, she stopped and put her hands on my shoulders. "Benny, if you ask the Lord for something, believing He will do it, then He will do it."

But my mother was also well aware of my poor marks in elementary school, and she proceeded to let me know it would also take a lot of work on my part.

"You will never become a doctor if all you do is watch television," she said one morning as she snapped off *The Three Stooges.* "You and your brother had better start reading something."

She insisted that we read at least two books a week. "Don't you touch that knob, Benny," she'd order if ever she caught me reaching for the TV. "Read your book."

And so I did, and the more I read, the more interesting books became. Before long I was devouring them.

Within two years I rose from the bottom of my class to the top. My good marks won honors in high school, which earned me a scholarship to Yale University, then the University of Michigan Medical School, and eventually helped me realize another long-held dream, a staff appointment at Johns Hopkins Hospital.

But how easily none of these things might have happened.

One of the problems I had as a kid was my violent temper. It was so severe that when it exploded I'd even attack others with a rock, brick, or anything else at hand. No matter how hard I tried to control it, my temper would snap like an old rattrap.

One day when I was fourteen, a boy in our neighborhood was tormenting me. Suddenly everything flashed red. Snatching a big camping kinfe, I lunged fiercely at his stomach.

Crack! The steel blade snapped as it struck his heavy metal belt buckle.

As the boy fled in terror, something also snapped in me. I was shocked at what I had nearly done: I might have killed that boy. Sickened, I stumbled home where I shut the bathroom door and slumped on the porcelain tub, staring at the wall.

How could I help myself? I knew that my temper was out of control. Something had to be done.

At that time in church we'd been reading the book of Proverbs. It was my favorite book—as it is now. As I sat on the edge of the tub, some of Solomon's words began to form slowly in my mind: "He that hath no rule over his own spirit . . ."

I couldn't help but feel that there was meaning for me in those words: "He that hath no rule over his own spirit is like a city that is broken down, and without walls" (25:28 KJV).

They were meant for me; I knew now for certain that I had to get control of my spirit. If I didn't, I'd end up in jail or dead.

"Ask the Lord, Benny, believing that He will . . ." Mother had said again and again.

Right then and there I knelt on the bathroom floor.

"Oh, Lord," I prayed, "take away my temper. I know, I believe You will."

And He did. There wasn't anything gradual about it at all. The Lord took away my temper, just like that. Whenever I'd feel it begin to boil, it would somehow simmer down as if someone had turned off the burner. I was in awe at what had happened to me, and I remained so.

When the time came to operate on little Christopher Pylant, I looked at my hand, the one that wielded the knife that fateful day, and I gave thanks that it was about to guide what I hoped would be a lifesaving scalpel.

That morning in the operating room, after I'd opened the back of Christopher's little shaven head, it was just as I expected: malignant dark tumor everywhere. I couldn't even see the brain stem, which evidently had been consumed by the cancer. Without the brain stem, there is no real life.

We excised as much of the tumor as safely possible, closed the incision and had the boy taken to the intensive care unit.

As I stepped into the waiting area, the parents rose with expectant faces. I didn't have the heart to tell them there was no hope, but I had to.

"I'm sorry we couldn't help your son," I said. "I know you both have prayed and I have prayed too. But sometimes the Lord works in ways we don't fully understand."

The mother and father did not flinch. Both still maintained that earnest look of conviction.

"Doctor," the father said as his wife nodded in agreement. "The Lord is going to heal our son. We're standing on his promise."

Taking a deep breath, I could only add, "Your faith is admirable."

I felt so very sorry for the Pylants who believed so strongly in something so hopeless. What I had seen in Christopher's brain was irrefutable.

However, three days after the operation something strange happened. Though Christopher was still comatose, his eyes began focusing and his physical movements began improving.

"Let's repeat his CT scan," I said, a peculiar feeling going through me.

As I studied the scan printout, I was amazed to see a tiny threadlike remnant of brain stem.

We had to go back in.

The next day, Christopher was back in surgery and I was again working on that discolored malignant tissue with scalpel and forceps. But where it had seemed so impossible to define planes before, I was suddenly able to lift the mass away in layers. I became excited. A nurse wiped perspiration from my brow as I worked. At last, after cleaning out all the crevices, there it lay, the healthy gray brain stem, intact, but flattened and distorted.

Within a month our patient was ready to leave the hospital. With Christopher smiling up at us, his parents and I thanked the Lord together. As they walked out of the hospital, the glory shone on their faces, and I heard my mother telling me once again: "If you ask the Lord for something believing He will do it, then He *will* do it."

Take My Hand

BETTY R. GRAHAM

My favorite hymn is "Precious Lord, Take My Hand," which has been special to me for many years. Recently, I heard it on the radio, and it brought back the memory of when it first became my favorite.

When I was five years old (a long time ago) and living in Lansdowne, Maryland, a suburb of Baltimore, my parents regularly went to an outdoor market in Baltimore—Holland Market. Dad had heard of it when he worked in the roundhouse at the B&O Railroad. It was close to that railroad station so many years ago. Every Saturday he and Mom would go there to get fresh vegetables for our family. It was a temporary market and only open on Saturdays. Farmers from the nearby farms would bring their produce to be displayed and sold at the crude stalls they set up each week. The market filled a whole city block, which was closed to traffic on market day. Stalls lined each side of the street, and people came from all over to purchase the fresh produce.

Mom and Dad always went alone to the market, but I constantly begged them to take me with them. Usually they refused to take me but one Saturday, they gave in. I was thrilled to be going marketing with them.

"You can come with us," Mom said, "but you must hold my hand and not get tired and whine to come back home until we finish our shopping."

"Oh, I will! I will! And I won't get tired," I cried and hurried upstairs to find a nice dress to wear. I could hardly wait to get there. I didn't have the chance to go many places. With five older brothers and sisters, there was always someone who could watch me if my parents went out.

My excitement built up as we passed places I had not seen before, so by the time we reached the market, my spirits were soaring. Dad parked the car and we all got out and started to walk down the street between the colorful stalls. The farmers called out their prices and quality to tempt buyers to their stalls. I had never seen anything like it.

It was Mom's routine to walk from one end of the market to the other, noticing the produce for sale and comparing prices in her mind before she even stopped to buy anything. Holding her hand, I trotted along beside her, proud as a peacock, and sure in my mind that everyone we passed could tell how grown up I was. Having reached the other end of the street, Mom turned to walk back, stopping from time to time to examine the tomatoes, corn, or lettuce on display. Of course, as she concentrated on her purchases, she had to let go of my hand, and one time I didn't reach to hold it again. Mom bought some corn, paid the seller, and handed the package to Dad to carry.

We then resumed our trek down the street, with me walking along a little in front of Mom. I felt so smug and confident as I strutted on my own in the "big city." I noticed some other small children with their parents, but they all hung close to their mothers, some even clutching the mother's dress. It made me feel superior to them. I could walk on my own. I wasn't afraid. I was a big girl.

Suddenly, I turned to speak to Mom, but she wasn't there. *Where was she? Had they finished their shopping and gone home without me?* I panicked and started to run through the market, crying and yelling at the top of my voice. I ran all the way to the other end of the market before someone grabbed me from behind. Terrified, I turned to look at the angry face of my father, who had chased me the length of the market, and who was panting from the exertion. And then I felt embarrassed. I didn't feel so grown up anymore. I knew I was in trouble. I had let go of Mom's hand and marched to my own drummer. Mom and Dad probably would never let me come with them again. But even with those negative thoughts, I felt safe. My father had found me. I wasn't lost after all.

I have carried that thought with me for the rest of my

life. When I was grown I knew that there was always a Father who would protect me—my heavenly Father.

That's why the chorus to the hymn "Precious Lord, Take My Hand" by Thomas Dorsey is still my favorite:

Precious Lord, take my hand, lead me on, let me stand,
I am tired, I am weak, I am worn;
Thru the storm, thru the night, lead me on to the light;
Take my hand, precious Lord, lead me home.

God Who?

NAN MCKENZIE KOSOWAN

During our teen years she'd been only a little shorter than I. But at this moment, in that big bed, she looked small and fragile. I was spending my regular day with my dear friend Ann this last summer of her life. Cancer, ravaging her body, couldn't touch her quick wit or beautiful smile.

"Sit down on the bed here beside me," she said. "Tell me what's happening in that interesting life of yours. Then I have some news to give you and some questions to ask."

In our teens I'd always looked up to "big sister" Ann as the most intelligent, attractive, charming girl I knew. I was always the one asking Ann questions. Now she was saying she had questions for me. This day there was a sense of expectancy in the air that I couldn't quite get a fix on.

Lord, I prayed under my breath, *I know You see whatever's going on from beginning to end. You lead. I'll follow.*

Even while I was sharing the happenings of my week with Ann, I was remembering how dramatically our relationship changed after we headed off for the university.

When we both married, we almost drifted apart as our common ground developed furrows of different outlooks, attitudes, and preferences. As our young families visited in earlier days, a distinct alienation between our interests, passions, and purposes began to show up. And then there was the mockery.

The mockery came when her husband, Phil, grabbed the opportunity to make snide remarks whenever anything about our new life in Christ came up. And it did come up. When Jesus is your life, He's a natural part of your conversation. I was devastated as Ann looked on with amusement when Phil would mock any reference to the Lord.

When my husband and I took our dismay to the Lord in prayer, He spoke, as it were, into our hearts, telling us to just keep on loving them. "They don't understand. Go ahead and live your life in Me in front of them. My grace is there for the mockery and the insults. Let those pass over your heads; they will not affect you. Be on the watch for where I will lead that you might not miss any turns."

We did experience God's grace, and Phil's clever, searing remarks did pass over our heads without effect. That was true of our kids as well. Passionate about their relationship with Jesus and the people He brought into their lives, they looked forward to our times with Phil and Ann's family. They accepted the way they were and loved them for Jesus, no matter what.

During one of those family visits, Ann read an article I'd written for a Christian *God Who* publication and asked me about my own relationship with Jesus and His people that obviously meant so much to me. That encouraged me until a mutual friend told me to watch what I told Ann. It seemed that on coffee breaks together, Ann often made fun of what I had shared with her.

When I asked the Lord about this, He gave me the same admonition as before: to just keep on loving them. I thought, *I'll do that until God tells me something more.*

Those Tuesday visits that last summer with Ann were precious. Of course, Jesus was as natural a part of my conversation as ever. Ann's responses indicated a curiosity about life in Christ, but she never suggested she was interested in trying it for herself.

Lord, I asked Him after one such visit particularly marked by a barrage of her questions, *when she keeps asking such imperative questions, why can't she respond to my answers?*

I wasn't expecting His answer, "Her husband is her god."

With that truth echoing in my mind, I prayed silently as I sat beside her on the bed, *Lord, I believe You would have me bind the influence of that idol in her life. So standing on that passage in Matthew 16:19 that says "Whatever you bind on earth will be bound in heaven," I do that now in the name of Jesus!*

There was a difference this day. Ann's questions were thoughtful and very moving. She wanted to hear about the life that starts with Christ here and now and continues after death. They were especially poignant in light of the news of her doctor's latest report. It said her death was imminent, probably before the end of the month. I remember few details of our final time of sharing, but I do remember she asked a question that could only be answered by introducing her to Jesus as Savior and Lord.

Ann prayed with her whole heart to receive Jesus into her life. Together we wept joyful tears and embraced: two sisters in Christ at last.

When Phil came home from work, he was surprised to see my car in the driveway. "Nan, you're still here! Where did you leave my dinner?" he called up the stairs.

"Come see," I laughed. "You sweethearts deserve a fancy dinner together. It's set up here tonight."

He bounded up the stairs, kissed his wife, and grinned at dinner spread out with lace and best dinnerware, hers on a bedside tray, his on a small table nearby.

When Phil let out a salacious remark (his way to compliment a woman) it went in my one ear and out the other as usual.

But this time it was different for Ann: no chuckle, no little smile. She raised her frail self on her poor thin arms and said in a no-nonsense tone, "Don't ever speak to Nan like that again."

I was quiet as I went downstairs to take up the meal for Ann and Phil. But inside my heart, bells were ringing: *Phil's no longer her god! God is!*

I stayed to clean up the kitchen and was blessed by the happy chatter coming from the bedroom above.

Ann died the next week with Phil by her bedside, holding her hand.

Phil was committed to the hospital himself with a fast-moving cancer close to the first anniversary of Ann's death. He told me he was prepared to follow his sweetheart; the sooner the better, as life had been so empty without her. Days later, a friend, who was a *God Who* professional colleague, prayed with Phil to accept Jesus as his Lord and Savior.

It sounded like a fairy tale where two sweethearts are united again in death. But it was no fairy tale. It was a true story of God's love triumphing, as caring friends were obedient to share with them the hope of glory in the good news of Christ.

Hope Across the Miles

KAREN KINGSBURY

Charles Herch had two brothers, but he never knew either of them. The first died at birth. And the second died tragically at age four. Although he grew up something of an only child, Charles never forgot how much his parents had lost.

"Don't worry, Mom," he'd tell her when he was a young teenager. "You'll always have me around. I'm never going anywhere."

Charles's mother, Katie, would grin sadly at her son and tousle his golden-brown hair.

"The good Lord has taken two of my boys home to be with Him," she'd say. "But He knows how much a person can handle, Charles. You're the boy He left for me and your father."

But when Charles turned eighteen, he was sent overseas to serve in the Korean War. The idea of losing Charles on a battlefield thousands of miles from home terrified his parents, but they prayed constantly for their son and believed God would protect him.

"Please, God, let us know when he needs our prayers,"

Katie would pray each night. "And bring Charles home safely to us. He's all we have left, Lord."

A year passed, during which Charles wrote to his parents as often as he could. He told them of the loss of life and the dangers he faced each day. And he asked them to keep praying for his safety.

Then on July 28, 1953, Charles was working with other infantrymen from the 2nd Infantry Division near a hill known as Outpost Harry. Charles had suffered minor injuries two days earlier, and was attempting only light duty until he was completely recovered.

It was midday, and Charles sat down for a rest some twenty feet from a supply center where the ammunition from their outpost was stored. There were grenades, shells, and other explosives.

"Hey, you're slacking off again, Herch," Ralph Dunn called out, grinning. He and a few of Charles's closest friends were standing near the ammunition taking a break. They knew that Charles had been injured, but they always enjoyed teasing each other.

"No more than you do every day of the week, Dunn," Charles retorted quickly, laughing at his buddies.

At that instant there was a terrifying explosion. Something had ignited one of the pieces of ammunition, and the entire supply area disintegrated into a ball of fire.

Ralph and four young infantrymen standing near him were killed instantly. Ten others, including Charles, were critically wounded. Bodies lay about the ground, and Charles groaned as he tried to feel where he was injured. He felt a gaping hole on his right side, and also along his neck and face. Despite the smoke and fire nearby, he was unable to move.

"Help me," he called out, his voice weak and raspy. "I'm dying over here. Someone help me."

Another soldier from his division heard him, and saw that he was bleeding badly from his injuries. He called for help, and another man joined him. Together they slid Charles onto a stretcher and ran him into an open field.

"Wait here, man," one of them shouted above the roar of confusion. "Someone'll be here soon."

Then Charles was alone. He drifted in and out of consciousness, and realized that he was bleeding to death.

"God, please don't let me die here," he whispered. "My folks need me, God."

At the same exact moment, across the world in Hamtramck, Michigan, Katie Herch sat up straight in bed screaming.

"Charlie, wake up!" Her voice was frantic and her husband shot up in bed, his eyes wide and disoriented.

"What is it, Katie?" he asked breathlessly.

"It's Charles. He's hurt; I have the feeling he needs our help."

Charlie Herch sighed and relaxed somewhat. "Katie,

he's in Korea. There's no way you could know whether he was in trouble or not."

Katie nodded emphatically. "Yes, Charlie, I prayed that God would let me know when he needed our help."

Charlie frowned. "What can we do, dear, even if he *is* in trouble?"

Katie's voice returned to normal and she sat up even straighter. "We can pray for him."

Charlie nodded and took his wife's hands in his. "Okay, let's pray."

Katie bowed her head and closed her eyes as she began to pray out loud. "Lord, You've woken me from a sound sleep. I just know it's because Charles is in trouble somewhere. I don't know what he needs or where he is, Lord, but You do. Please help him, God. Whatever he needs, please provide it. In Your holy name, amen."

Back in Korea, at that same instant, Charles heard a distinct voice speaking very near his ear.

"Don't worry. You are not going to die today. This is not the time or way for you."

Charles looked around, but he was completely alone in the field. The realization sent chills down his arms and he knew that the words were true, whoever had spoken them. He felt himself relax, and in a matter of minutes, a helicopter landed, whisking him off to a local military hospital.

Not until two days later did Katie learn what had happened to her son. An officer came to their door and told them that Charles had been injured but was recovering.

"When was he hurt, sir?" Katie asked, feeling the hair on her arms begin to rise.

The officer looked at his information sheet. "It says here he went down July 28, sometime around two o'clock in the afternoon."

Katie quickly figured out the time difference and realized that what she suspected had been true. God had indeed heard her prayers and directed her to pray for Charles at the exact moment of his need.

An Advance from God

EMILY DOWNS

I'm a freelance writer and as any starting writer (and probably many veterans) will tell you, writing is not a get-rich-quick job. I have more than once been told that if I want to make a living, don't become a writer. Not much has changed over the centuries, those trying to live "by their pen" as the illustrious Jane Austen, have never had an easy time of it. We pour out our hearts and souls, but for what? Pittance! Only top writers can actually make a substantial living off their writing. Well, I am in the first flush of my freelance writing career and as you can imagine, I am quite poor, despite some early success.

When my husband and I struggle to pay our bills, I often reassure myself that this gift is from the Lord and I am using it to bring glory to Him. I love my work and have been regularly selling pieces to *Brio* and *Encounter* magazines. I have a real heart for teenagers struggling to live like Christians in this difficult culture. Along with going to school and trying to send out freelance work I am also working on a book. Although, article sales help, over the past year I have often given into depression over our financial state. I often need the Lord to assure me that I am following His path by choosing writing over a consistent paycheck. It seems that I am supposed to write, because every time I feel like burning my grammar books something happens; like landing a six-article deal or being the recipient of yet another writing award.

However, the other day, I thought my writing career had met its end. I was working away on my old used computer—literally held together with duct tape—when the keyboard quit working. My poor overused computer had been in the shop just a month ago for the very same reason. At the time I was told that my keyboard was going, but I prayed that the Lord would just miraculously keep me afloat. I was very familiar with this road, having been down it too many times before. My used computers were always breaking down and leaving me with no way to work. Needless to say, with looming deadlines and lost writing days, I would become very emotionally distraught. Feel hopeless.

With a sinking heart I called the computer shop and tried to keep back my tears as I learned that replacing the keyboard would cost more than the computer was worth. I hung up in utter despair. This computer was third in a line of used, slightly abused writing instruments that had already caused me much distress over the past two years. A piece-by-piece computer breakdown would be like someone trying to go to the office and time after time finding it closed with no explanation or promise of reopening. It's unnerving and stressful, wondering when you will be able to get your work done. It was nothing short of a nightmare—without a computer I was finished! Not only could I not work, I couldn't send out any manuscripts to my editors. My computer was my office, my work, and my very indispensable companion—we were inseparable!

I called my husband with shaking hands to tell him the news. He listened as I explained what had happened. We discussed trying to get my computer fixed again, but we both knew it was a waste of money.

Finally, he said in a flat voice, what both of us had been thinking, "We just don't have the money to get you a new computer right now."

I knew it hurt him to say the words, but if the money's not there, it's not there.

By this point I had given in to the growing dread in my soul and the tears prickling my eyes. I hung up the phone and cried letting my anger and fear surface. *Why me? Wasn't I writing for the Lord? Hadn't He given me this gift to use for Him?* I was so upset. I tried to call my mom but she didn't answer. I started to dial a friend's number, a newer friend whom I normally wouldn't call in such desperation, when I suddenly realized I had cried and complained, but not once had I stopped to ask the Lord for help. I put down the phone and told the Lord what had happened and how I felt. I told Him I couldn't write without a computer. "Is this the end?" I asked. I also asked for the grace to handle whatever His plan was for me and my writing.

I continued with the phone call to my friend. When I got her voicemail I poured out my heart and then apologized for leaving such a crazy message.

She called back a few minutes later.

I started to say I was sorry for bothering her with my problems when she interrupted me to say she was sitting in my driveway.

"Really?" I said peering out my front window to see her car.

We sat in her car and talked for a while. After a few minutes she handed me a folded paper.

"I hope this doesn't offend you, but I set some money aside six months ago to use for the Lord."

I looked at her blankly.

"I have been praying about this money and every time I do you come to mind," she explained.

I shook my head slowly, understanding, "Oh, I can't."

"I really believe in your writing," she continued. "Reading your articles has helped me, and I know they have and will help others. I really care about the issues you write about, and I want to support your writing."

I didn't know what to say; my mind was spinning with her words.

"I was going to just slip the money in your box at church, but when I got your call I knew now was the time. This way you can use the money toward a new computer," she said.

Fresh tears rolled down my cheeks as I humbly thanked her and we hugged. When I got inside, I opened the check and discovered that it was enough money to buy a new computer! I sat on the kitchen floor, crying yet again. In utter amazement I realized what was happening. I had told the Lord about my broken computer and ten minutes later someone showed up at my door with a check for a new computer! I had always said that if I ever sold my book, the first thing I would buy was a new computer. But the Lord, through my sweet friend, had given me an advance. Clearly the Lord wanted me to continue with my writing and depend on Him to provide every step of the way.

As we all experience from time to time, it is often more difficult to trust in things unseen (impossible really without the Holy Spirit). I have more than once wondered if my prayers were really heard. I've often thought it would just be so much easier if we could see God and hear His voice. Although I have yet to see or hear God with my eyes and ears—I have experienced His handiwork. When I cried out to the Lord, He answered me.

Psalm 116:5–7 says that the Lord is gracious and merciful and we can rest in Him because He deals bountifully with us. The Lord has a plan for our lives. His plan included my being able to continue writing. Romans 8:28 says that all things work together for good for those who love the Lord and are called according to His purpose. If we are seeking and obeying God's will for us—which we discover through prayer and the reading of God's Word—we can wholly trust in Him to provide a way for us to continue along that path, even when things seem impossible, like writing without a computer! I think my computer broke so the Lord could show Himself to me in a very real and personal way.

I am so humbled by God's grace: how often are prayers answered so quickly and so specifically? My new computer was nothing short of a miracle!

A NOTE FROM THE EDITORS

This original book was created by the Books and Inspirational Media Division of Guideposts, the world's leading inspirational publisher. Founded in 1945 by Dr. Norman Vincent Peale and his wife, Ruth Stafford Peale, Guideposts helps people from all walks of life achieve their maximum personal and spiritual potential. Guideposts is committed to communicating positive, faith-filled principles for people everywhere to use in successful daily living.

Our publications include award-winning magazines like *Guideposts, Angels on Earth,* and *Positive Thinking,* best-selling books, and outreach services that demonstrate what can happen when faith and positive thinking are applied to day-to-day life.

For more information, visit us online at www .guideposts.org, call (800) 431-2344, or write Guideposts, 39 Seminary Hill Road, Carmel, New York 10512.